To: Gisel

Don't wait
loved ones vanish, or the economy
collapses before reading this book.
Know that Jesus loves you. He died
for you. You are precious to HIM.
Hold on to the promises GOD has
for you today.

GOD BLESS You!

PROMISES PROMISES PROMISES

BY MICHELLE T. FORD

Published by
In Search Of The Universal Truth (ISOTUT) Publisher
ISOTUT Books
Denver, Colorado USA

Promises, Promises, Promises
By Michelle T. Ford

Copyright © 2011 by Michelle T. Ford

All rights reserved. No part of this book may be reproduced by any means or in any form whatsoever without written permission from the Author and the Publisher, except for brief quotations embodied in literary articles or reviews.

Cover Design By Trevor Ford

First Edition
First Printing June 2011

ISBN 13: 978-1-61500-010-4
ISBN 10: 1-61500-010-0

Library of Congress Control Number: 2011924700

Visit our website
www.insearchoftheuniversaltruthpublisher.com

Publisher info.
In Search Of The Universal Truth Publisher
8822 E. Florida Ave. Unit 114
Denver, Colorado 80247, USA

Contents

    God Reveals a Promise..7
    Believing God's Promises..14
    How to Use This Book..23
1. Promises of Answered Prayer....................................25
2. Promises of Blessings..32
3. Promises of Christ's Return..39
4. Promises of Encouragement......................................55
5. Promises of Everlasting Life......................................63
6. Promises of Excellence..73
7. Promises of Forgiveness..82
8. Promises of Freedom..90
9. Promises of Growth..98
10. Promises of His Presence...107
11. Promises of Joy..115
12. Promises of Love...123
13. Promises of Peace..132
14. Promises of Salvation...140
15. Promises of Strength..150
16. Promises of the Holy Spirit.....................................158
17. Closing...169
18. Other Promises of God..173
19. Romans Road to Salvation.....................................175

Dedicated To

The Most High God, my Heavenly Father who has inspired me to walk in His way and will, remaining with me to see it through as promised.

Bishop Dr. Al Baxter for the rema word and his wife, Mrs. Dalice Baxter, for her kind words. Both have been an encouragement and support.

Shawntelle, my daughter for believing in me.

My mother, Glenfield for teaching me about values and unity.

My second mother, Vivian and my dad, Kenneth, pillars in my life.

Michael, my brother and friend and his wife, Heather for their help in all circumstances.

GOD REVEALS A PROMISE

Staring out my living room window as I sat on my couch alone, I could hardly admire the glimmering stars on God's dark canvas. I felt numb and distant. The ups and downs of life's recent events seemed to have worn out any measure of joy, sadness, excitement or disappointment.

Turning to the Bible on my lap, I aimlessly flipped through the pages, wondering what to study next for my quiet times with the LORD. After doing this for about ten minutes, the silence was softly interrupted by a male voice asking, "What about my promises?" Surprised that somebody else was in the house, I responded, "What was that?" I thought I must be hearing things so I dismissed it and continued. About five minutes later I heard the voice ask again, "What about my promises?" Now I knew I wasn't hearing things nor was this my imagination. The LORD was speaking to me, as he had done many times before. *"My sheep listen to my voice; I know them, and they follow me"* (John 10:27).

I pondered this question for a while and reflected on where I was in my life: my husband, Trevor and I had just separated and what comfort that was left in the house was devoured by strife and quarrelling with my teenage daughter, Shawntelle. It seemed like there would never be any peace. I felt abandoned by God, my husband and my daughter. My whole world was spinning out of control. I needed strengthening from God.

In hopes that the next random page would be an answer, I thought, "Let me just read the first thing that my eyes see."

For I know the plans I have for you, says the LORD, plans to prosper you and not to harm you, plans to give you hope and a future.

Jer. 29:11

I thought, "Really!? Was this God's plan of prosperity and not to harm, because I was hurting! Future and a hope? At some point and time LORD, you might want to fill me in on what that would look like!" I had to really read that scripture again, again and yes, again. Then the revelation came to me as I realized that I was looking at my situation through human eyes, so God helped me to see with spiritual eyes reminding me that, *"His thoughts are not my thoughts, neither are my ways His ways"* (Isaiah 55:8). With things in better perspective, He revealed another promise to me:

Being confident of this, that He who began a good work in you will carry it on to completion until the day of Christ Jesus.

Philippians 1:6

He will finish the good work that he started in me and my life. He had not abandoned me after all. I just need faith to see outside of my current circumstances that this wasn't the end. Here was the first of many of God's promises that I could hold on to and that he would use to sustain me, not only for this trial but for others to come.

With this new revelation, I began to study and apply God's other promises in my life. Over several months, my spirit became rejuvenated, restoring the joy and peace that had been lost. God didn't change the circumstances, but he changed me. My troubles didn't seem to matter and the downward spiral quickly became an upward ladder to my spiritual restoration. As I continued to read and give God praise for His precious promises, my life began to take on a whole new meaning as I began to feel the presence of God once again.

God, You Want Me to Write a Book?

I shared these changes with Bishop Dr. Al Baxter, who is the Senior Pastor at Faith Miracle Temple, the church I attend in Toronto. He has been supportive and encouraging through my circumstances and I just wanted him to know how the LORD was working through my quiet times.

Bishop then gave me what I believe to be a rema word from the LORD (a spoken word from God). He suggested that I compile these quiet times into a book. "This will be a very helpful book and a tremendous blessing to many in the body of Christ", he said emphatically. My reaction at first was, "Well, why didn't the LORD tell me to turn it into a book himself? I mean, He was the one who told me about His promises in the first place." Then I thought about my ways. Would I have done it if He had told me Himself? This isn't just about the LORD and me in private; now it involves other people. So the answer: probably not.

As the weeks passed, I felt convicted in my own spirit to do this, which to me was a confirmation that this was from the LORD. So now I would write the book, not because of my great ability but simply because the LORD asked me write it. I had hopes that it would not only be a blessing to those in the body of Christ, but also to those who do not yet know Jesus. If the LORD is calling me to do this with an open door, I should run directly through.

I had considered myself to be insignificant and not influential at all by society's standards. I thought to myself, "LORD, could I really be helpful?" Then God reminded me of the imperfect people in the lineage of the perfect Jesus, the Saviour of the world: Moses was a murderer, yet God used him to deliver His people out of Egypt; David defeated Goliath the giant as a youth, only to later commit adultery with a married woman named Bathsheba, covering it up by having her husband killed. It wasn't God's will for these men to sin, but He chooses the imperfect things of this world to fulfill His perfect will (1 Corinthians 1:27). God told Moses, "I will be with you" (Exodus 3:12); He told David, "I have been with you wherever you have gone" (2 Samuel 7:9). It was never about what these people were capable of doing for God. In the same way I thought it was about me, as my insecurities and faults crept up, but it's not. It's about what God will do through me for His glory and His purpose.

After realizing this, I stopped listening to those poisonous whispers from the enemy about what I was incapable of doing. I slammed that door and crushed the fear and doubt right out of my thoughts and started typing away. This book is the result of that faith in God.

God Fulfills a Promise

With a new hope in the promises of God, I believed He would work out the situation for my good. Many nights I was on my hands and knees pouring out my heart to Him. I prayed about my marriage and specifically asked God that if it was His will for us to reconcile, that it would to be at Faith Miracle Temple. If it was there, I wouldn't feel awkward since it's a comforting place where I worship the LORD. In faith, I wrote this prayer down in my journal so I could later see the fulfilled promises of God.

Having no way of contacting my husband, I hung on to His promises of answered prayer. Ten months later and by divine appointment, I walked into the church sanctuary with Shawntelle and she turned to me and said, "Mom, there's Trevor." Shawntelle calmly walked over to say hello, but I had to rush outside in the muggy August heat to catch my breath as I remembered my prayer to God. I praised the LORD and laughed until my face was hurting! Collecting myself as best I could, I calmly walked back into the service, knowing the worship was about to begin. Shawntelle had already invited him to sit with us.

This was the beginning of the restoration and the LORD has been strengthening our relationship and marriage ever since. I still had to persevere through some trials along the way but I was in the LORD's hands. God's promise was fulfilled when my husband moved back just over a year later.

God Fulfills another Promise

Before this, I was already several months into fervent prayer concerning my daughter. She was a typical teen: quarrelsome at every opportunity, disrespectful, selfish and unwilling to help around the house. I earnestly prayed to God to change her heart, save her from herself and the direction of darkness that she was clearly heading. Looking at myself, I asked God to give me the patience to endure and to still be a loving mother towards her. I had also asked the Lord to let me examine myself if I am where the fault lies and to change me. Just because we're parents doesn't make us perfect.

God heard my prayers and a year and a half later, Shawntelle did a complete turn-around, from not wanting to anything that related to God in any shape or form to putting her faith in Jesus and being baptized. Now she too wants to reach out to the youth and draw them closer to God. This was only a couple weeks after Trevor first came to my church, so he was also able to attend the ceremony (The LORD's timing is perfect).

We are all a work in progress and there are more obstacles to overcome, but now I am reminded of God's promise that He who has started a good work in me is well able to finish it. Amen.

Believing God's Promises

Today, it's apparent that we are living in times of false and broken promises. We see it from governments, workplaces, corporations, churches and even our own friends and family. Broken promises of lower taxes, the raise at work that didn't happen or the miracle diet product that didn't work; that failed financial windfall or the family member that didn't come through when you needed them most.

Noted author George Orwell wrote, "In a time of universal deceit, telling the truth is a revolutionary act." The devil has worked hard sowing lies and broken promises in every area of our life, for he is the father of lies (John 8:44). His purpose is not only to bring strife and division, but ultimately to instil doubt into our hearts about the important promises of truth found in God's word.

Many have allowed him to succeed. It's startling how many people I have met who are believers in Jesus but are in such great despair: weary, worn-out and unsatisfied; financial troubles, broken marriages and rebellious children. Out of work and nearly out of hope.

Have we allowed the false promises of the world to take the place of God's promises without even realizing it? False promises that finding the perfect mate will fill the lonely void, that money and success will bring satisfaction or that a happy family means a nice house, car and lots of gadgets. Exhaustively working and raising the children only to find that at the end of if it all, television and video games have replaced the parental nurturing that they truly need. Some kids fall subject as we turn on the television and listen to the news or read the papers about youth violence, bullying and teen suicide. On the other spectrum, we have those who are out of work or losing their jobs as the economy fails and discouragement, distrust and the harsh realities of life set in. The one thing that they have forgotten is that God has the final say and His promises can be trusted. We need to hang on to the promises that God has for us, holding on to His unchanging hand. When all other ground around us is sinking sand, He will save us from these terrible times (Luke 21:36).

In contrast of the natural tendency for the devil to lie, it is *impossible* for God to lie at all (Yes, there is one thing that's impossible with God!):

God did this so that, by two unchangeable things in which it is impossible for God to lie...

Hebrews 6:18

Tomorrow will be even worse: a time of great tribulation coming on all nations, such as not been since the beginning of the world and never will be again (Matthew 24:21). Jesus even said that unless those days are shortened, all flesh will die (Matthew 24:22). Even though there will be an opportunity to still make it into heaven, declaring that you believe in Jesus will be marking yourself for physical death (but not spiritual death): "Then you will be handed over to be persecuted and put to death, and you will be hated by all nations because of me" (Matthew 24:9).

Bibles may be outlawed then as hate literature, so take hold of God's promises today as you walk in His grace and mercy and your days ahead will be brighter.

If you have already put your faith in Jesus, there will one day come a time when we will return home to heaven to be with the LORD, in the twinkling of an eye (1 Thessalonians 4:16-17). This is known as the "Rapture", the vanishing of God's people.

Not Seeing is Believing

Now faith is being sure of what we hope for and certain of what we do not see.

Hebrews 11:1

"I'll believe it when I see it", is a common phrase used today. Yet, faith is the complete opposite. In fact, if we choose to walk by physical sight alone, deliberately ignoring this type of faith, we cannot please God. Hebrews 11:6 says, "And without faith it is impossible to please God, because anyone who comes to him must believe that he exists and that he rewards those who earnestly seek him."

In Genesis chapters 15 to 22, we read the story of how God promised an old shepherd named Abraham, offspring as numerous as the stars in the sky (Genesis 15:5). Yet he was childless and his wife, Sarah was barren (Genesis 11:30, 17:17). But there would be a testing of faith and perseverance for the promise to be fulfilled.

Believing God's Promises

Abraham was seventy-five years old when the LORD first promised to make him into a great nation, yet he had to wait until he was one hundred years old until his only child, Isaac was even born – that's 25 years (Gen 12:1-4, 21:5)! God then specifically told Abraham that it would be through Isaac that His promise of countless descendants would be realized (Genesis 21:12). Yet, in seemingly complete contradiction, God told Abraham to offer his only son as a sacrifice! This wasn't a newborn - Abraham had some years to come to love his son as he was a young man, or a "lad" at the time God asked this. Despite this contradiction, Abraham obeyed. Why would he do this?

By faith Abraham, when God tested him, offered Isaac as a sacrifice. He who had embraced the promises was about to sacrifice his one and only son, even though God had said to him, "It is through Isaac that your offspring will be reckoned." Abraham reasoned that God could even raise the dead, and so in a manner of speaking he did receive Isaac back from death.
Hebrews 11:17-20

Now consider Abraham's extraordinary faith in God's promise at that time: today, it's common to believe in a resurrected Jesus and there's at least one story about a dead boy being brought back to life in the Old Testament, before Jesus (2 Kings 4:32-36), but Abraham had no such history to draw from as far as we know. Yet, Abraham was not swayed by human reasoning or circumstances. Rather, he had faith in God who he believed could raise his son from death.

So Abraham set out to do exactly as God asked (Genesis 22:9-14). Knowing Abraham's intention to fully obey Him, God stopped him from sacrificing his son at the last moment. He then provided an alternate sacrifice, a ram that was stuck in the thickets nearby.

After God saw Abraham's faith and obedience, the fulfillment of the promise was then complete:

> *The angel of the LORD called to Abraham from heaven a second time and said, "I swear by myself, declares the LORD, that because you have done this and have not withheld your son, your only son, I will surely bless you and make your descendants as numerous as the stars in the sky and as the sand on the seashore. Your descendants will take possession of the cities of their enemies, and through your offspring all nations on earth will be blessed, because you have obeyed me.*
>
> *Genesis 22:15-19*

Even before Abraham had fully obeyed, God had already spoken the reality of the promise fulfilled:

> *As for me, this is my covenant with you: You will be the father of many nations. No longer will you be called Abram; your name will be Abraham, for I have made you a father of many nations. I will make you very fruitful; I will make nations of you, and kings will come from you.*
>
> *Genesis 17:4-6*

God told Abraham that "you will be" and "I have made you" the father of many nations at the same time. To God, it was already a reality waiting to happen.

We see our life as a movie, where things are revealed to us one frame at a time. We can only watch the beginning, middle and end as it happens. But God sees our life as a complete painting on a canvas, where everything past and present exists at the same time. To Abraham, the fulfillment of the promise was yet to take place, but to God it already existed. To God, it already happened – it was already a reality. All Abraham had to do was to believe God and obey.

The book of Hebrews also refers to Abraham's faith in God's promises. It encourages God's people to stay faithful through the example of Abraham's faith in God's promises:

> *God is not unjust; he will not forget your work and the love you have shown him as you have helped his people and continue to help them. We want each of you to show this same diligence to the very end, so that what you hope for may be fully realized. We do not want you to become lazy, but to imitate those who through faith and patience inherit what has been promised.*

> *When God made his promise to Abraham, since there was no one greater for him to swear by, he swore by himself, saying, "I will surely bless you and give you many descendants." And so after waiting patiently, Abraham received what was promised.*

People swear by someone greater than themselves, and the oath confirms what is said and puts an end to all argument. Because God wanted to make the unchanging nature of his purpose very clear to the heirs of what was promised, he confirmed it with an oath. God did this so that, by two unchangeable things in which it is impossible for God to lie, we who have fled to take hold of the hope set before us may be greatly encouraged. We have this hope as an anchor for the soul, firm and secure.

Hebrews 6:10-19

Through faith, by perseverance and obedience we inherit the promise. There may be a time of waiting, praying and perseverance. At times God will require us to wait, pray and persevere through a trial until He opens a door. Other times he will require us to also put our faith into specific action to test our obedience.

Two unchangeable things: God's promise and oath. We all know how the terms of contracts and services are always changing. We sign up for one type of cell phone plan, only to get a surprise charge three months later. It's the same with credit cards, bank account fees, TV service, etc, etc. There's always a disclaimer that says they can change the terms of the deal anytime and usually not for our benefit. It doesn't seem to matter if we honour our part of the agreement or not.

But the Bible says it's impossible for God to lie, neither does he change the terms of His covenant

(Malachi 3:6). Once he's made a promise, he can't change it, add to it or cancel it at anytime. It's not just valid for only 6 months and then the price goes up, it's valid forever! We have the complete Word of God today – there won't be an updated version coming down from heaven with any new changes, ever.

His promises are an anchor for our soul. An anchor is essential to keep a ship firmly stationed not only in calm waters but in stormy seas. With no anchor it would be dashed upon the rocks and destroyed. In the same way, God's promises are an anchor for our souls at all times. Peter calls them His very great and precious promises; that's how important they are for our faith (2 Peter 1:4).

Don't Just Try it – Live it

True faith isn't something we *try* but a *way of life*. There's a quote that says, "I don't believe in diets, but I believe in changing my lifestyle". Diets offer a temporary change, but a lifestyle change is permanent. Faith is the same thing. If you get conviction and pray, pray, pray until something happens, I guarantee that you will see the LORD show up in your life. Don't look at your situation or circumstance by what you see, no matter how bad or hopeless it may seem. Instead, as Abraham did, against all hope, believe in hope (Romans 4:18). Against all reason, believe in hope. Against all feelings, believe in hope!

Nothing is impossible for God and we are to "live by faith, not by sight" (2 Corinthians 5:7). Faith is to look with spiritual, not physical eyes.

How to Use This Book

I hope these promises will be as useful to you as they are for me. I look back and reflect on the promises of God every day, thanking Him for where I am in my life and where I have come from. Anytime I need a reminder or some encouragement, I know that God is always faithful and His words can be trusted.

My hope is that as you too will also reflect on God's promises and what He's done in your life. At the end of each chapter there are two blank pages: "My Circumstances" and "My Praises". As the title of the first one says, you can just write down what's going on in your life as it relates to that particular chapter. Then under My Praises, you can praise the LORD for where you are and what you want to see changed. Begin to praise God in relation to your situation. If you tend to write a lot or plan on lending the book to others, you can leave these sections blank and start a personal journal instead.

As you reflect on the days, weeks and months gone by, you will see your life changing right before your eyes, beginning to see God in a completely different light. His promises won't change, but your situation will.

When you read about my situations and personal praises written in this book, none of the testimonies had come to pass yet; these praises and promises were from 2008. I read them daily and hung on to them, taking God at His word while speaking it in faith. I am now rejoicing that I have a testimony to share with you so that you can see the manifestation of God in your own daily life.

Be encouraged to know that we are all precious to God and He wants to be a part of your life if you let Him. I hope that as you read further into the book that your life will be transformed and hope renewed. At the end of each chapter I have written what God has promised in His word followed by my praises to Him in regards to His promises. These examples should help you get started and reconnect you to opening the channel to a Heavenly Father that loves you dearly. Dig in to the promises of God and substitute the negative words of your current reality for praises in what you believe God wants manifested in your life.

May the LORD bring to light the promises He has in store for you as He has done for me. I would also encourage you to check the Bible for yourself to see if what I am saying is true. Good reading and God bless you.

1 Promises of Answered Prayer

If you believe, you will receive whatever you ask for in prayer.

Matthew 21:22

God hears us when we pray. He hears our words and hearts. We are confident that when we come before God, we don't minimize Him, but *maximize* Him. God loves when we depend on Him to guide our paths and involve Him in the decisions that affect our daily lives.

Stop doubting and believe. God wants to open up many doors in our favour, but we limit Him when we do not seek Him or do not believe that He will do as we have asked. Some may pray with little faith, saying, "Well LORD, if it's possible" or "it would be nice if..."

Be specific. Call out the person's name in which you want God to heal or to be saved. When praying for your children, call them by name. Describe the thing or situation that is afflicting you and pray for the LORD to deliver you from it, whether it's depression, addiction, lust, envy, etc. There are many things that can keep us in bondage and it is time that these chains are broken.

Believe you have already received it. When our prayers line up with God's word and His will for our lives, there is nothing that can stop it, except you. Change your posture and get in a position to receive the blessings that God has for you today.

Persevere in prayer. Don't give up after one prayer, one week, a month or a year. Keep pressing on. Remember, it can take years to get in the predicament or bondage you are in and change can take time. Some things God will fix right away and some things will be a process as He changes us from the inside out. Leave your problems with God; He doesn't need your help. If He needed our help then don't you think you would have been able to change yourself already? Be diligent daily and on your knees often, continuing to pray, pray, pray until something happens. Get in the word, and get to know the One you are speaking to. Don't give up on God because God will never give up on you. Never! So He is worthy of our praises.

PROMISE

O, you who hear prayer, to you all people will come. When we were overwhelmed by sins, you forgave our transgressions. Blessed are those you choose and bring near to live in your courts! We are filled with the good things of your house, of your holy temple. You answer us with awesome deeds of

righteousness, O God our Saviour; the hope of all the ends of the earth and of the farthest seas.
Psalm 65:2-5

PRAISE

LORD, I am blessed that you hear and listen to my prayers. You treat me with love and compassion, for this is your nature. Thank you for choosing to bring me near to live in your courts.

You have forgiven my transgressions and have filled me with the good things of your house. You have answered me with awesome deeds of righteousness. O God my Saviour, my hope will remain in you until the very end. Amen.

PROMISE

Ask and it will be given to you; seek and you will find; knock and the door will be opened to you. For everyone who asks receives; he who seeks finds; and to him who knocks, the door will be opened. Which of you, if his son asks for bread, will give him a stone? Or if he asks for a fish, will give him a snake? If you, then, though you are evil, know how to give good gifts to your children, how much more will your Father in heaven give good gifts to those who ask Him?
Matthew 7:7-11

PRAISE

LORD, I am blessed that you have provided me an open channel to you, to be able to ask for things that will bring you glory and honour. If I knock, the door will open and you LORD, will not open a door that would cause me harm. I trust that you have my best interests at heart. May doors be opened that fulfill a purpose in my journey to draw me nearer and closer to you, LORD. Help me to discern your open doors and let me walk through them with confidence in you. I thank you, LORD, for the instruction to seek and find. Father, when I search the things of you, I can be assured of clarity and have no doubt that what I find is of you and from you. Amen.

Father, I believe that what you say is true and I have received in anticipation the things I have asked for: a restored/ strengthened marriage/ relationship in you LORD. I believe and receive a successful career in my endeavours that glorifies you with the faith given me, that I can be respectful and holy in the job/ task at hand in a powerful way that will set me apart. I believe and receive the travels that I will take and the mission work I will do shall bring glory to you, LORD. I believe and receive strengthening in Jesus name. Amen.

PROMISE
For the eyes of the LORD are on the righteous and his ears are attentive to their prayers; but the face of the LORD is against those who do evil.
1 Peter 3:12

PRAISE
LORD, my heart is at peace to know that your eyes are on me. When you look at me you do not see the flesh, but you see the Holy Spirit which you have deposited in me and the righteousness of your Son. You

hear and listen to my prayers, like a loving Father does with his children when they come to him. There is nothing that I can do that would separate your love from me. Those that try to bring me down, your face will be against them. They do evil in your sight. I am yours O LORD, and they shall not have victory over me. May I fervently seek your Son, for it is by His blood that I have been washed clean. Amen.

PROMISE
This is the confidence we have in approaching God: that if we ask anything according to his will, he hears us---whatever we ask---we know that we have what we asked of him.
1 John 5:14-15

PRAISE
Father, I pray that what I have asked for is in your will for my life. I approach you in confidence that these things have already been done on my behalf, providing that they are in your will. I wait with great expectation and your perfect timing. I thank you my LORD, for giving me what I have asked for; my marriage restored, my daughter saved, to win souls for the glory of the kingdom of heaven and mission work in which I will help those in need and lead them to you. (Substitute with your career, health, healing, peace, etc as you approach God). Amen.

Promises of Answered Prayer

MY CIRCUMSTANCES

MY PRAISES

2 Promises of Blessings

From the fullness of his grace, we have all received one blessing after another.
John 1:16

God wants to bless us. Throughout the Bible, God has shown many examples of how He enjoys blessing His children. In the beginning, God made a covenant with Abraham and told him that through him all the nations would be blessed. Abraham was a man not in his youth, yet the LORD blessed him with a son. From that one son came many descendents who were also blessed, having many livestock, fine gold, long life and God's protection and love. That same God still lives today.

It's not what He will give us, but what He's already done for us. Render your heart out to Him. We cannot do the right things for the wrong reasons. Be genuine, authentic and real.

Be obedient to the LORD. When we are obedient to His word in our lives and in our worship to Him, it will give birth to blessings. He who knows the righteous desires of your heart will give you every spiritual blessing and make you whole. If we are willing and obedient, we will eat the best from the land (Isaiah 1:19). That means blessings in our household, family, finances, spirit, healing and the like.

> *Do not merely listen to the word, and so deceive yourselves. Do what it says. Anyone who listens to the word but does not do what it says is like a man who looks at his face in a mirror and, after looking at himself, goes away and immediately forgets what he looks like. But the man who looks intently into the perfect law that gives freedom, and continues to do this, not forgetting what he has heard, but doing it—he will be blessed in what he does.*
>
> James 1:22-25

PROMISE

May the LORD bless you from Zion all the days of your life; may you see the prosperity of Jerusalem, and may you live to see your children's children.
Psalm 128:5-6

PRAISE

Father, I praise you for this great blessing that will continue down from generation to generation. Your Son may soon return, yet you O LORD are able to fulfill your blessings at any time. For to you a day is like a thousand years and a thousand years are like a day. I receive your blessing and will watch it grow for generations to come. Lord Jesus, I am blessed every day in you with the breath of life and the promise of salvation. You provide for me in abundance. I eagerly await blessings to come. Amen.

PROMISE
I will bless them and the places surrounding my hill. I will send down showers in season; there will be showers of blessing.
Ezekiel 34:26

PRAISE
Father, I praise you to know that there is a season for everything and everything for a season. May I be drenched by you with showers of blessings and goodness; your goodness LORD, is like manna from the heavenly realms, and I know that I will be more than satisfied. Amen.

PROMISE
From the fullness of his grace, we have all received one blessing after another.
John 1:16

PRAISE
Father, your grace is sufficient. I receive one blessing after another, as you have not passed judgement on me as my sins deserve. The greatest blessing given to me was sending your only Son to die on the cross that I may be saved. Thank you LORD for the blessings I have received and the ones that are to come. Amen.

PROMISE
And we know that in all things God works for the good of those who love him, who have been called according to his purpose.
Romans 8:28

PRAISE
Father, I know that what I am going through now and over the last few days, months or years doesn't seem good. Yet, in all of this I know and believe that you work for the good in all things. You never promised that everything would be good, for you said in this world we will have troubles. But you LORD have overcome the world, so I know that through my circumstances good will come out of it. Whatever path that might be or I might take, I look forward to the good it will bring. But in the present I rejoice and will be glad in it as I await the good that will manifest from it. I thank you LORD for loving me and being mindful of me, a sinner saved by grace whom you love and who loves you. Amen.

PROMISE
Praise be to the God and Father of our LORD Jesus Christ, who has blessed us in the heavenly realms with every spiritual blessing in Christ.
Ephesians 1:3

PRAISE
Father, I am blessed to know what I have been given in Christ and how powerful that has made me in you. As every spiritual blessing in Christ is developing, I can go

boldly and without fear and be blessed. No matter what I do in Christ to advance the gospel and win souls, it is not by my strength but yours. No matter what I say in Christ, it brings life and bears fruit, for you give me the words to say and I am blessed. Father, I thank you for every spiritual blessing in the heavenly realms: the joy, the peace, the healing, the prosperity, the wisdom, the knowledge, the guidance, the favour and so much more in Jesus name. Amen.

MY CIRCUMSTANCES

MY PRAISES

3 Promises of Christ's Return

Men of Galilee; they said "why do you stand there looking into the sky" This same Jesus, who has been taken from you into heaven, will come back in the same way you have seen him go into heaven.
Acts 1:11

We need to be ready for the return of Jesus. When Christ left the earth, He said that He would one day return again and take us with Him. As we are now living in the last days, we eagerly await our LORD's return, knowing that He will fulfill this promise. We need to make sure that we are ready at His coming and not caught sleeping and unprepared like in the parable of the Ten Virgins:

At that time the kingdom of heaven will be like ten virgins who took their lamps and went out to meet the bridegroom. Five of them were foolish and five were wise. The foolish ones took their lamps but did not take any oil with them. The wise ones, however, took oil in jars along with their lamps. The bridegroom was a long time in coming, and they all became drowsy and fell asleep.

> *At midnight the cry rang out: "Here's the bridegroom! Come out to meet him!"*
> *Then all the virgins woke up and trimmed their lamps. The foolish ones said to the wise, "Give us some of your oil; our lamps are going out."*
> *"No," they replied, "there may not be enough for both us and you. Instead, go to those who sell oil and buy some for yourselves."*
> *But while they were on their way to buy the oil, the bridegroom arrived. The virgins who were ready went in with him to the wedding banquet. And the door was shut.*
> *Later the others also came. "Lord, Lord," they said, "open the door for us!"*
> *But he replied, "Truly I tell you, I don't know you."*
> *Therefore keep watch, because you do not know the day or the hour.*
>
> *Matthew 25: 1-13*

The bridegroom was a long time in coming. People feel the same way today, as if Christ will never return. Every generation has been waiting for Him to come back and yet it has not happened in their time, so some become complacent and figure there's plenty of time. "I'll prepare later" or "I have so many other things to think about right now". We go on living and carrying on as usual thinking, "This will never happen in my lifetime, either", and so most are not prepared. But then, when we least expect it, the cry rings out, "Here's the bridegroom! Come out to meet him" and "with a loud command, with the voice of the archangel and with the trumpet call of God" (1 Thessalonians 4:16). I don't want people to be deceived, because the ten virgins, represented purity yet five were foolish and five were wise. The foolish were not able to enter in, so let us examine ourselves, even those who say, "I know the LORD", and prepare ourselves to enter in.

Jesus has left us signs of His coming. This is indicative of the period of time that this generation today is living in. We have always had wars, earthquakes and famines, but there is an increase in frequency and intensity. Wars are escalating to nuclear proportions while the flooding and disasters are no longer isolated to the third world nations. Famine will hit North America, so don't be deceived by thinking we are exempt. Nation will rise against nation and Kingdom against kingdom; these things are happening right before our very eyes. Look at Tehran, Egypt and now Libya. Increasingly violent earthquakes in various places such as Haiti, New Zealand, and Japan. Just turn on the television and witness the destruction.

> *As Jesus was sitting on the Mount of Olives the disciples came to him privately. "Tell us," they said, "when will this happen, and what will be the sign of your coming and of the end of the age?" Jesus answered: "Watch out that no one deceives you. For many will come in my name, claiming, 'I am the Christ', and will deceive many. You will hear of wars and rumours of wars, but see to it that you are not alarmed. Such things must happen but the end is still to*

come. Nation will rise against nation and kingdom against kingdom. There will be famines and earthquakes in various places. All these are the beginning of birth pains. Then you will be handed over to be persecuted and put to death, and you will be hated by all nations because of me."

Matthew 24:3-35

This is why I said in the beginning of the book, that telling people in those days that we are a Christian is marking ourselves for death. Christians will be seen as people of hate and intolerance, not of love. The persecution has already started from people now correcting us during the "holiday" season by telling us that it is not appropriate to say, "Merry Christmas". In the workplace, it is already discouraged or a violation of policy to talk about God, with consequences resulting in a reprimand or dismissal. In some countries such as China, India and Pakistan, it could cost you your very life.

If millions of people have already vanished from all over the world, then this is the beginning of the Tribulation period. Watch the behaviour of the people around you; even those close to you will betray you if you have put your faith in Jesus Christ as your Saviour:

You will be betrayed even by parents, brothers and sisters, relatives and friends, and they will put some of you to death. Everyone will hate you because of me. But not a hair of your head will perish. Stand firm, and you will win life.

Luke 21:16-17

Being a believer in Jesus at this time will mean that you may be arrested, brought to trial or even killed. Do not worry beforehand about what to say. Just say whatever is given you at the time, for it will not be you speaking, but the Holy Spirit (Matthew 10:19-21). Remember your hope is not on this earth but in heaven.

After the vanishings, which is when Jesus has come back for all of those who have made Him their Lord and saviour, the government may try to force people to get a chip in their hand or forehead in order to buy and sell:

He also forced all people, great and small, rich and poor, free and slave, to receive a mark on their right hands or on their foreheads, so that they could not buy or sell unless they had the mark, which is the name of the beast or the number of its name. This calls for wisdom. Let the person who has insight calculate the number of the beast, for it is the number of a man. That number is 666.

Revelation 13:16-18

All of your personal information would be stored on this tiny chip, including bank accounts, medical information, etc. They may even tell you that it is so they will be able to track you and keep a census in case more people vanish. This technology is already in operation today through a tiny implantable Radio Frequency

Implantable Microchip (RFID) called VeriChip, from the Positive ID corporation[1].

This chip is not of God but of the Satan (the Beast). There will be a false sense of peace and security for three and half years. This will be the antichrists' and Satan's turn to reign and cause terror upon the earth. You will then be forced to take the chip or as it is called in the Bible, "the mark of the beast", on your forehead or hand, or possibly be put to death. Whatever you do, no matter what the circumstances DO NOT get this mark, for that is your one way ticket to hell and there is no turning back once you have accepted it (Revelation 13:8,14:11). Call on Jesus and ask for him to forgive your sins, and come in to your life and to be your LORD and personal Saviour. That is why I am stressing the importance of being ready now like the wise virgins.

> *He (Satan), was given power to make war against the saints and to conquer them. And he was given authority over every tribe, people, language and nation. All inhabitants of the earth will worship the beast-all whose names have not been written in the book of life belonging to the Lamb that was slain from the creation of the world. He who has an ear let him hear. If anyone [1]is to go into captivity, into captivity he will go. If anyone is to be killed with the sword, with sword he will be killed. This calls for patient endurance and faithfulness on the part of the saints.*

---

[1] **Verichip implantable ID chip: http://www.positiveidcorp.com/about-us.html**

He (Satan) exercised all the authority of the first beast on his behalf, and made the earth and its inhabitants worship the first beast' (this would be the antichrist, Satan's right hand) whose fatal wound had been healed. And he performed great and miraculous signs, even causing fire to come down from heaven to earth in full view of men. Because of the signs he was given power to do on behalf of the first beast, he deceived the inhabitants of the earth. He ordered them to set up an image in honour of the beast who was wounded by the sword and yet lived. He was given power to give breath to the image of the first beast, so that it could speak and cause all who refused to worship the image to be killed
Revelation 13:7-10, 12-15

I don't tell you these things to frighten you but to prepare you to be able to recognize the truth when you see these events unfolding before your very eyes, that you and your loved ones may be saved.

But before all of this happens the LORD says that there will be a time when many will turn away from the faith and will betray and hate each other (Matthew 24:10, 12). People say that there is more than one way to get to heaven, turning to pagan gods and witchcraft thinking that, "I am a good person. I will go to heaven when I die." These are all lies of Satan trying to get you to depend solely on your own devices and turn away from the one true God. None of us are good, for if we were good, Christ wouldn't have had to die and His death on the cross would have been in vain (Romans 3:10, 23). Christ died so that we would be spared from the wrath is to come, that we would receive forgiveness for our sins (1 Thessalonians 1:9-10). When He came down from heaven, was nailed to the cross, shed His blood and died, he made full payment for our sins both past, present and future. I assure you there will be no good people in heaven, but heaven will be full of sinners who have been saved by grace and faith in Christ Jesus alone.

*Hundreds of m*illions of people and *all* of the children, including those still in their mothers tummies will be taken from every nation; vanished. These are the ones who have been spared from what is to come. I know that some might be saying, "Many people from generation to generation have been waiting for this rapture to happen and it didn't. They have since died, and life still continues on the same way and people are still waiting":

Brothers and sisters, we do not want you to be uninformed about those who sleep in death, so that you do not grieve like the rest of mankind, who have no hope. For we believe that Jesus died and rose again, and so we believe that God will bring with Jesus those who have fallen asleep in him. According to the Lord's word, we tell you that we who are still alive, who are left until the coming of the Lord, will certainly not precede those who have fallen asleep. For the Lord himself will come down from heaven, with a loud command, with the voice of the archangel and with the trumpet call of God, and the dead in Christ will rise first. After that, we who are still alive and are left will be caught up together

with them in the clouds to meet the Lord in the air. And so we will be with the Lord forever.
1 Thessalonians 4: 13-17

Now, brothers and sisters, about times and dates we do not need to write to you, for you know very well that the day of the Lord will come like a thief in the night. While people are saying, "Peace and safety," destruction will come on them suddenly, as labor pains on a pregnant woman, and they will not escape. But you, brothers and sisters, are not in darkness so that this day should surprise you like a thief. You are all children of the light and children of the day. We do not belong to the night or to the darkness. So then, let us not be like others, who are asleep, but let us be awake and sober. For those who sleep, sleep at night, and those who get drunk, get drunk at night. But since we belong to the day, let us be sober, putting on faith and love as a breastplate, and the hope of salvation as a helmet. For God did not appoint us to suffer wrath but to receive salvation through our Lord Jesus Christ. He died for us so that, whether we are awake or asleep, we may live together with him. Therefore encourage one another and build each other up, just as in fact you are doing.
1 Thessalonians 5:1-11

If you are reading this book and people have already vanished and Bibles are scarce or outlawed as hate literature, then hold on to this book for dear life. If you have the Bible, it will tell you what to look out for now.

So when you see standing in the holy place (in Jerusalem) the abomination that causes desolation, that will be the antichrist, let the reader understand—then let those who are in Judea flee to the mountains. Let no one on the roof of his house go down to take anything out of the house. Let no one in the field go back to get his cloak. How dreadful it will be in those days for pregnant women and nursing mothers! Pray that your flight will not take place in winter or on the Sabbath. For then there will be great distress, unequalled from the beginning of the world until now—and never to be equalled again. If those days had not been cut short, no one would survive, but for the sake of the elect those days will be shortened. At that time if anyone says to you. "Look here is the Messiah! or, "There he is, out in the desert, do not go out; or "Here he is, in the inner rooms!", do not believe it. For false Christ and false prophets will appear and perform great signs and miracles to deceive even the elect –if it were possible.

See I have told you ahead of time. For as lightning that comes from the east is visible even in the west, so will be the coming of the Son of Man. Wherever there is a carcass, there the vultures will gather. Immediately after the distress of those days the sun will be darkened, and the moon will not give its light; the stars will fall from the sky, and the heavenly bodies will be shaken. At that time the sign of the Son of Man will appear in the sky, and all the nations of the earth will mourn. They will see the Son of Man coming on the clouds of the sky with power and great glory. And he will send his angels with a loud trumpet call, and they will gather his elect from

the four winds, from one end of the heavens to the other. Now learn this lesson from the fig tree: As soon as its twigs get tender and its leaves come out, you know that summer is near. Even so, when you see all these things, you know that it is near, right at the door. I tell you the truth; this generation will certainly not pass away until all these things have happened.
Matthew 24:15-34

If you are ready, you will come back with Him, but if you refuse to know Him, you will still see Him coming in all of His glory. When Christ returns the first time, those who do not believe in Him will not see Him but you will know that He has come because of the vanishings. There will be no government, army, scientists or special intelligence that will be able to give a plausible explanation besides the truth. You may hear things like, "the people were abducted by aliens" or "this is the way the earth purges people because of over-population", or that it was nuclear weapons, etc. Lies! Lies! Lies! The truth is the rapture has come and gone. This is why I urge you to take hold and put your faith in Jesus now. He is the only one that can save you from what will come. To God be the glory.

PROMISE

In my Father's house are many rooms; if it were not so, I would have told you. I am going there to prepare a place for you; I will come back and take you to be with me that you also may be where I am.
John 14:2-3

PRAISE

Father, my heart was troubled but your words always ring true. You are my breath of fresh air every second, every minute and every hour. Your words are my comfort and my strength. My assurance is in the heavenly realms. Father, I am grateful that my place of rest will be with you. My spirit longs to be with you where you dwell. I am grateful that you are mindful of me LORD, that you have prepared a place for me, for you loved me first. My soul rejoices that one day, where you are I will be there also. I rejoice, I rejoice, for you are an awesome God. Amen.

PROMISE

Men of Galilee; they said "why do you stand there looking into the sky" This same Jesus, who has been taken from you into heaven, will come back in the same way you have seen him go into heaven.
Acts 1:11

PRAISE

Father, only you are worthy of such a magnificent and glorious departure when you had left us and in the same magnificent glory you will come back. When your feet touch down on the Mount of Olives and it has split into two, every eye shall see your glory and every eye shall see your honour. Every tongue shall give you the praise and we who believe shall be with you when you come. Amen.

Promises of Christ's Return

PROMISE

For the LORD himself will come down from heaven, with a loud command, with the voice of the archangel and with the trumpet call of God; and the dead in Christ will rise first. After that, we who are still alive and are lift will be caught up together with them in the clouds to meet the LORD in the air. And so we will be with the LORD forever.
1 Thessalonians 4:16-17

PRAISE

Father, the Rapture is something that I look forward to. What a grand exit. To be able to be caught up, that we may dwell with you rejoices my spirit. I know the time is coming near for these things to occur. Give me the faith and the strength LORD to be ready on that day and not be found wanting. To God be the glory. Amen.

PROMISE

Look, he is coming with the clouds, and every eye will see him, even those who pierced him; and all the peoples of the earth will mourn because of him. So shall it be! Amen.
Revelation 1:7

PRAISE

Father, the coming of your Son brings such excitement to my heart. He comes in his splendour like the true King of Kings and LORD of Lords. The sky is His chariot, His horses are the clouds and all eyes shall be on our Saviour. But we who have believed in you and have put our trust and faith in you LORD, know that your righteous judgement has come. But you will wipe away every tear, for you are righteous and holy in all that you do. Amen.

MY CIRCUMSTANCES

Promises of Christ's Return

MY PRAISES

4 Promises of Encouragement

You hear, O LORD, the desire of the afflicted; you encourage them and you listen to their cry.

Psalm 10:17

We are all meant to encourage and to be encouraged. What our reality may be today does not need to be our reality tomorrow. If we are feeling unloved, we can feel loved. If we are weighed down by guilt, we can receive forgiveness. If we are blinded in a cloud of confusion, we can experience God's guidance and wisdom. If our life is upside down in turmoil, God can turn it right side up and we can enjoy peace in your heart.

When we were infants and learning to walk we would take a few steps, fall and then contemplate in our minds, "maybe I should just stick to crawling cause this falling thing is getting played out" or "it's probably better if I stay close to the ground cause this falling down hurts". But because of the love and encouragement from our parent's kind words saying, "Come on you can do it!" or just that excited look on their faces and exclaiming, "You almost had it! Look, keep going!" That God-given drive of determination compels us to dust ourselves off and try again. God is the same way. He's always encouraging us to reach higher, strive for better, dream bigger and step out in faith.

God's word is full of encouragement and He will be there as we celebrate our victories. God loves His children and desires the best for them. If we do not believe that God is a loving God, or if we don't believe that, "...in all things God works for the good of those who love him, who have been called according to his purpose"(Romans 8:28), then we are probably not encouraged in our own spirit and we are unable to encourage others.

> *For those God foreknew he also predestined to be conformed to the image of his Son, that he might be the firstborn among many brothers and sisters. And those he predestined, he also called; those he called, he also justified; those he justified, he also glorified.*
> *Romans 8:29-31*

"What then, shall we say in response to this? If God is for us, who can be against us" (Mark 9:40)? But if we know that God is loving, forgiving and merciful who delights in sharing His goodness, then encouragement is within our grasp and we can share it to lift up others. As believers in Christ, God is always pleased when we build each other up with encouragement (1 Thessalonians 5:11). Whether we're reminding one another about the joy of the coming of the LORD, or cooking a meal for someone who is sick, or giving a hug or a smile to someone who is down, a little encouragement can go a long way to spur one another on toward love and good deeds (Heb 10:24-25). The most encouraging thing of all is that we are not alone: "For I am with you always, to the very end of the age" (Matthew 28:20).

PROMISE
You hear, O LORD, the desire of the afflicted; you encourage them and you listen to their cry.
Psalm 10:17

PRAISE
Father, what a great comfort it is to know that I am not alone in my afflictions. I trust and believe that you hear my cries. You encourage me with your words and bring comfort as I sing and cry out to you. You are a just LORD; righteous, holy and sovereign, and to you I will cling. You know my desires and I will wait on you. I know and am confident that every tear I shed does not go unnoticed, for you record every tear on your scroll (Psalm 56:8).

PROMISE
"For I know the plans I have for you", declares the LORD, "plans to prosper you and not to harm you, plans to give you hope and a future".
Jeremiah 29:11

PRAISE

Father, how refreshing and comforting it is to know that you have plans for me. I need not worry what comes my way for you O LORD are in control. I eagerly wait for your plans to unfold, knowing that they are not to bring me harm. Even if there are obstacles that I may face I am comforted because I can go through them in you, knowing and being reassured that I will prosper, for you LORD have given me a future and a hope. I will cling and hold on to your unchanging hand. I give unto you my life, my future, my thoughts and my family. Amen.

PROMISE

May God himself, the God of Peace, sanctify you through and through. May your whole spirit, soul and body be kept blameless at the coming of our LORD Jesus Christ.
1 Thessalonians 5:23

PRAISE

Sanctify me O, LORD; this is my prayer. For when I am in you and you are in me I will not be found lacking or wanting for anything when you come, for my spirit will be whole. Do with me your will in order that I shall be ready and kept blameless in spirit, soul and body on that glorious day. Amen.

PROMISE

May our LORD Jesus Christ himself and God our Father, who loved us and by his grace gave us eternal encouragement and

good hope, encourage your hearts and strengthen you in every good deed and word.
2 Thessalonians 2:16-17

PRAISE

Father, I am thankful that you love me; your grace continues to encourage and give strength. My hope is in you LORD, and the joy I feel in my heart grows daily, for you are an awesome God. Your words and deeds are righteous. Like a double edged sword your words penetrate my soul and I am convicted and lifted up. By your unfailing love I am comforted. Amen.

PROMISE

God is not unjust; he will not forget our work and love you have shown him as you have helped his people and continue to help them.
Hebrews 6:10

PRAISE

Father, even though I am unworthy, I am grateful that you see me as worthy through your Son; that you would allow me to serve you. I know you say that whatever we do for the least of these, we do for you. LORD you are just and holy; let me remain humble before you. Let my right hand not know what my left hand is doing when I help others. For the glory belongs to you and is yours alone. Amen.

PROMISE
But you are a chosen people, a royal priesthood, a holy nation, a people belonging to God, that you may declare the praises of him who called you out of darkness into his wonderful light.
1 Peter 2:9

PRAISE
Father, I thank you for choosing me and caring for me as your own. I belong to you and I thank you for calling me out of darkness in to your light. For I lived in darkness far too long, separated from a relationship with you. You are my wonderful light that radiates from the depths of my heart and soul. Father, I praise your name. Hallelujah! For you are worthy of the highest praise. Glory and honour belong to you alone. Amen.

MY CIRCUMSTANCES

MY PRAISES

5 Promises of Everlasting Life

I give them eternal life, and they shall never perish; no one can snatch them out of my hand.

John 10:28

God desires to be with us for eternity. Can you fathom living for eternity where God Himself will dwell with us? In Revelation 21:1-27, we can get a small glimpse of what this eternity will be like: God will wipe every tear from our eyes and there will be no more death or mourning or crying or pain, (but there will be peace, joy, and laughter) for the old order of things will pass away. Jesus will make everything new again. Where the streets are paved with fine gold and the gates to the dwelling are made of pearls and other fine jewels. A river of water as clear as crystal and fruit trees yielding its fruit of every kind. "To him who is thirsty I will give to drink without cost from the spring of the water of life. He who overcomes will inherit all this, and I will be his God and he will be my children" (Vs. 6-7).

When we say yes to Jesus, we are moved from a place of darkness to light and we begin to be changed from the inside out. As the decades zoom by and our bodies begin to break down, the wear and tear of life can drag us down. Not so in heaven. Our bodies will be changed, and all things are new. No sickness, no sore backs, no deformities, broken bones, stiff or missing joints. No failing eye sight or hearing impairments. Hallelujah!

But, there is also an eternal dwelling place for those who remain separated from Christ. It wouldn't be fair if I did not share with those who choose to reject Jesus Christ. It is a place where there is pain, suffering and torment. "But the cowardly, the unbelieving, the vile, the murderers the sexually immoral, those who practice magic arts, the idolater and all liars-- their place will be in the fiery lake of burning sulphur" and, "Write this down for these words are trustworthy and true" (Revelation 21:5, 8).

God does not want anyone to go to hell. The LORD is not slow in keeping his promise, as some understand slowness. He is patient with you, not wanting anyone to perish, but everyone to come to repentance (2 Peter 3:9).

God originally prepared hell for the devil and his demons, not man. Then he will say to those on his left, "Depart from me, you who are cursed, into the eternal fire prepared for the devil and his angels" (Matthew 25:41).

Therefore, only the people who have rejected God and His Son Jesus will be the ones that will perish, because God doesn't send people to hell; they send themselves

by choice: "For God did not send his Son into the world to condemn the world, but to save the world through him. Whoever believes in him is not condemned, but whoever does not believe stands condemned already because he has not believed in the name of God's One and only Son" (John 3:17-18).

We have a choice while we are still alive to choose life and as long as today is still called today there remains hope. For when we die our fate is sealed and there are no second chances after death, there are only second chances in life.

There was a rich man who was dressed in purple and fine linen and lived in luxury every day. At his gate was laid a beggar named Lazarus, covered with sores and longing to eat what fell from the rich man's table. Even the dogs came and licked his sores. The time came when the beggar died and the angels carried him to Abraham's side. The rich man also died and was buried. In hell, where he was in torment, he looked up and saw Abraham far away, with Lazarus by his side.
So he called to him, "Father Abraham, have pity on me and send Lazarus to dip the tip of his finger in water and cool my tongue, because I am in agony in this fire." But Abraham replied, "Son, remember that in your lifetime you received your good things, while Lazarus received bad things, but now he is comforted here and you are in agony. And besides all this, between us and you a great chasm has been fixed, so that those who

want to go from here to you cannot, nor can anyone cross over from there to us."

He answered, "Then I beg you, father, send Lazarus to my father's house, for I have five brothers. Let him warn them, so that they will not also come to this place of torment."

Abraham replied, "They have Moses and the Prophets let them listen to them."

"'No, father Abraham", he said, "but if someone from the dead goes to them, they will repent."

He said to him, "If they do not listen to Moses and the Prophets (or their friends and neighbours, etc.) they will not be convinced even if someone rises from the dead."

Luke 16:19-31

Today we have all kinds of people witnessing about the gospel: from the church, your neighbours, coworkers and family members. Some witness on the streets, others through relationships or the media. Today, North America and most of the world is flooded with the word of God (Hebrews 8:11). There will be no excuses and we won't be able to tell God on that day, that we never knew.

Good or bad, rich or poor, slave or free, Jesus is the answer and the only way. The choice is ours to make, but our fate is also ours to endure. The time is now to choose life everlasting.

PROMISE

I know that my Redeemer lives, and that in the end he will stand upon the earth. And after my skin has been destroyed,

yet in my flesh I will see God; I myself will see him-with my own eyes I, and not another. How my heart yearns within me!
Job 19:25-27

PRAISE

Father, how great it is to know and believe that you my Redeemer lives. Redemption is yours alone in the sacrifice you have made just for me. You have given your life for me and in the end, even if it is to the grave I go to sleep, I await your rapture. Decay of my flesh is certain; I know that absent from my body I will be present with you LORD. But redemption, knowing and being sure that the purchase you have made through your sacrifice and shed blood on the cross, you will come to collect me, and redeem what you have purchased. Your face is what I long to see. Your presence is where I long to dwell. The spirit within me cannot contain itself as my heart overflows with joy. Amen.

PROMISE

For my Father's will is that everyone who looks to the Son and believes in him shall have eternal life, and I will raise him up at the last day.
John 6:40

PRAISE

Father, what a glorious free gift that you have given me, For when we believe in your Son, whom you have sent with such a grand reward and blessings of eternal life, those both past and present will not be disappointed, for your word is truth and your promises are everlasting. And as simple as this request is Father, there are many who cannot accept this truth, for it is too simple to comprehend. This grieves my spirit. I can just imagine that you who are spirit mourn deeply, for you don't want anyone to perish. We all belong to you and are your children and creation. Help and guide me O LORD, to share the good news. Amen.

PROMISE

I give them eternal life, and they shall never perish; no one can snatch them out of my hand.
John 10:28

PRAISE

Father, I thank you for reclaiming me, protecting me and allowing me to come to know the truth, for your truth has set me free. The enemy is always looking and seeking to devour me, and draw me back into the world and as appealing as it may seem at the time it all leads to emptiness and death. But to believe in your Son who has given me eternal life, it is you LORD I choose to follow. Help me to always be on guard; that it is your voice and your voice alone that this sheep hears. Your words are the hearing aids to my soul. To you, O LORD I will be forever grateful. Amen.

PROMISE

Listen, I tell you a mystery: We will not all sleep, but we will all be changed—in a flash, in the twinkling of an eye, at the last trumpet. For the trumpet will sound, the dead will be raised imperishable, and we will be changed.
1 Corinthians 15:51-52

PRAISE

Father, how privileged I feel that you share your mysteries with your children who will listen: the mystery of Christ in us. For on that great and blessed day when the trumpet is called, what a joyous time that will be. All my imperfections will be made perfect. My hand that doesn't bend will bend like new. My back that pains me from injury will pain me no more. The person of old I will not be, for all will be made new thanks to thee! Blow, trumpet blow! Amen.

PROMISE

After that, we who are still alive and are left will be caught up together with them in the clouds to meet the LORD in the air. And so we will be with the LORD forever.
1 Thessalonians 4:17

PRAISE

Father, I thank you that you find me worthy of such a reception; to be caught up in the air to meet you. I have never flown unless it was by plane, but you LORD are majestic and full of splendour and this will be the one final travel that I look forward to. How great though art.

How great though art. Hallelujah Lord Jesus! How great though art. Amen.

MY CIRCUMSTANCES

Promises of Everlasting Life

MY PRAISES

6 Promises of Excellence

Commit to the LORD whatever you do, and your plans will succeed.

Proverbs 16:3

God wants us to do our best. One thing we know is that we serve an excellent God, and He wants His children to be excellent and excel in the things that they do. When we commit our families, our jobs, career goals, relationships and our finances to God, He will always find the most excellent way to work things out for our good. Whatever we do, He wants us do our best at it. Whether we're washing up dishes in the restaurant, be the best dishwasher you can be, or pumping gas at the gas station – wash the windows and offer to check the oil too. If we're making incisions on the operating room table, or building the next satellite to go into orbit, offer your best to God (Genesis 4:3-5). No matter what career or job you are doing, He expects your best. Work as if you are working for the LORD not men (Colossians 3:23-24).

Our attitude will help to propel you to where you want to go, but it must always start with God. We limit ourselves at times with insecurities and doubts: "What will others think if I do this" or "Maybe now is not the right time to take chances with something new". Or procrastination: "I've just got so much on the go right now, I really don't have the time to fit this venture in" or "I'll get to it next week or maybe next month." In turn we end up not striving for what we want. Make our requests known to God and "in all your ways acknowledge Him, and he will make your paths straight" (Proverbs 3:6). That doesn't mean that everything we want He will do because it may not be what is best for us. He knows us better than we know ourselves. However, if what we want lines up with His will, He will make a way for it to come to pass.

We have desires in our heart that are bursting to come out but have fears stopped us from fulfilling them? There are things that God will put on our heart to do. The only one who will stop them from them coming to pass is us. Satan will always whisper lies to persuade us away from the will of God. He knows that if we give God a chance to move in our life, we will become more powerful and a threat to him because now we are in a position to influence others for God. But when we suppress those desires and refuse to step out in our talents, we continue living unfulfilled lives, never realizing the magnitude of where God wants to take us. We may eventually give way to bitterness and hatred of our existence. Then everyone that comes across our path may experience that discontentment and wrath.

God expects us to use our talents to serve others. If we are happy with the position in life that we are in, and the blessings we have in the LORD, then Amen. Continue to do what we're doing in the most excellent way that will bring God the glory. As we continue to shine, the promotion and favour will follow. But, if it is time for us to fulfill our dreams and plans God has for us, then pray about them, with specifics. God hears us, so believe that He hears.

God will start to open our heart and eyes to the new possibilities very clearly if we listen. Put your request before God, then talk to other people about that request. Seek advice from elders, pastors, and people in the church or who you are close to. These should be positive, encouraging people who are doing well in the LORD themselves. Don't forget that God speaks through people as well, so try to listen. If we have two or more people saying the same thing regarding what we have shared with them, then we're probably getting confirmation. If two or more agree then you can feel safe to step out (Matthew 18:19-20).

Remember to start with God first. When He starts opening doors, they will open up to a whole new realm of opportunities that no man can shut. We just have to be willing to walk through the door and leave the fear behind, for it is not of God, for He did not give us a Spirit of timidity, but a Spirit of power, of love and of self-discipline (2 Timothy 1:7). Perfect love drives out fear so begin to trust in God. Remember that if adversity lurks its evil head, God is right there in our corner to bring us through, for He is more than able. Those are the doors that God will close and no man can open, so be blessed and step out in the most excellent way!

PROMISE

Be strong and very courageous. Be careful to obey all the law my servant Moses gave you; do not turn from it to the right or to the left, that you may be successful wherever you go.
Joshua 1:7

PRAISE

Father, I thank you for equipping me with strength and courage. For you did not give me a Spirit of timidity but one of strength. Your instruction is clear: to walk the straight and narrow road, for to my left and to my right Satan is always lurking and wants to devour me. Help me to boldly stay on the narrow path and give me the faith it takes that I may be successful wherever I go. Amen.

PROMISE

Commit to the LORD whatever you do, and your plans will succeed.
Proverbs 16:3

PRAISE

Father you have provided me with a foolproof plan to commit everything to you and I will succeed. Your word is truth I believe and receive what you say. Help me not to get in the way of myself, for you don't need my help. My story has already been written by you for me. Just help me to enjoy the road which is my journey with a happy ending in your kingdom. Amen.

PROMISE
Not so with you. Instead, whoever wants to become great among you must be your servant, and whoever wants to be first must be your slave—just as the Son of Man did not come to be served, but to serve, and to give his life as a ransom for many.
Matthew 20:26-28

PRAISE
Father, I am so grateful that you came to give us an example and show us who is truly great among you. For I know that what I do for the least of them, it's as if I were doing it for you. To be served here on earth leaves earthly reward, but to serve others on earth means a reward in the heavenly realms, for these are the things my Father sees. Amen.

PROMISE
I tell you the truth, anyone who has faith in me will do what I have been doing. He will do even greater things than these; because I am going to the Father.
John 14:12

PRAISE
LORD, give me the faith and the courage to go forward, knowing that you are in my corner. You advocate for me and you're the way to the Father. I receive the great things you have for me to do. I trust in

you LORD that my faith will continue to be strengthened as I follow your lead. Amen.

PROMISE

I no longer call you servants, because a servant does not know his master's business. Instead, I have called you friends, for everything that I learned from my Father I have made known to you. You did not choose me, but I chose you and appointed you to go and bear fruit—fruit that will last. Then the Father will give you whatever you ask in my name.
John 15:16-16

PRAISE

Father, I am so grateful that you chose me because I know where I would be right now if you hadn't. I would still be living in the dark, still going about my old ways of partying, smoking and the like, still walking in ignorance. You Lord Jesus have called me "friend". You have shared with me the intimate things that your Father has taught you, that I too may call him Father. I pray to go forward and bear fruit, fruit that will last. Your word has lasted through the test of time and will continue to endure forever. I believe that what I have asked for in your name has already been done and I'm just waiting for the time when you will reveal it. Amen.

PROMISE

What, after all is Apollos? And what is Paul? Only servants, through whom you came to believe as the LORD has assigned to each his task. I planted the seed, Apollos watered it, but God made it grow.
2 Corinthians 3:5-6

PRAISE

Father, I know that it was you who drew me to yourself. You changed my heart even though I knew of you and believed in you, though not intimately at the time. The seed that was planted from hearing your word; seeing the difference in those whose lives you had touched was the watering. This allowed that love for you and the desire within me to grow. Only you LORD, could do this, for no man or person has filled me the way you have. I follow you, the author and finisher of my faith. For I am just dust and ashes, and you will always be my Gardener who quenches my thirst.

Promises of Excellence

MY CIRCUMSTANCES

MY PRAISES

7 PROMISES OF FORGIVENESS

All the prophets testify about him that everyone who believes in him receives forgiveness of sins through His name.

Acts 10:43

One of the most precious things that Christ has given us is His life crucified on the cross. When the world was at its worst in sin, Christ died for us knowing that His act of love would not only reconcile us to the Father, but that we would receive forgiveness of our sins. The blood He shed still covers us till this very day.

Jesus' arrival here on earth ushered in a new way for people to relate to God. Christ brought salvation to show us the way to the kingdom: forgiveness for a sinful people and freedom to those who are in bondage. There was no longer a need for ongoing sacrifices. "Christ died once for all, the righteous for the unrighteous, to bring you to God" (1 Peter 3:18). In June Hunts' book entitled, "How to forgive when you don't feel like it" she makes a good point when she said, "From our vantage point, we

Promises of Forgiveness

can scarcely understand how blessed and fortunate we are to live on this side of the B.C/A.D dividing line. Before Christ, forgiveness was not permanent and the blood sacrifices had to continually be repeated. Then, because of Christ's life, death, and resurrection, He gave to believers in Him forgiveness that is free, complete, and irreversible. How tragic that many are still living as though we are on the B.C side, as though full forgiveness, permanent forgiveness still cannot be found; as though Christ has still not come."[2]

God's forgiveness isn't for one time, even if we continue to mess up. His blood covers our past, present and future sins: a multitude (1 Peter 4:8). But if we refuse His act of love on the cross and don't believe that He died for our sins, then, we will remain separated from a relationship with God. If we try to put our hope in our "goodness", we will also bear the full price for our sins through punishment and torment in hell. Isn't it easier to believe in Him and be covered by His precious blood, then to take a chance with our soul only to find out after we're dead? Then it's too late for the "could of, would of, and should of," but didn't. There is no going back once our fate has been sealed. Are we making excuses? Are we willing? Remember this: God's willingness to forgive us will never end, but our time here on earth will end (Hebrews 4:6-8). To God be the glory.

---

[2] **How to forgive when you don't feel like it - Pages 51 & 52**

PROMISE

If my people, who are called by my name, will humble themselves and pray and seek my face and turn from their wicked ways, then will I hear from heaven and will forgive their sin and will heal their land.
2 Chronicles 7:14

PRAISE

Father, how great it is to be assured that when I come to you in humility, you are quick to hear my prayers. Father, I long to seek your face and walk in you who has called me by name. For I know that my sins are forgiven when I turn from my wicked ways. Make me whole O LORD, make me whole. Amen.

THE PROMISE

No longer will a man teach his neighbour; or a man his brother, saying "know the LORD" because they will all know me, from the least of them to the greatest, declares the LORD. For I will forgive their wickedness and will remember their sins no more.
Jeremiah 31:34

PRAISE

Father, I am grateful that you have shattered the high places so we may all come to know you. You have gone out in to the world to declare the good news to all who will follow, and receive you. Thank you for forgiving me my sins for they were/are many and remembering them no more. Amen.

PROMISE

The LORD is compassionate and gracious; slow to anger abounding in love. He will not always accuse, nor will he harbour his anger forever; he does not treat us as our sins deserve or repay us according to our iniquities. For as high as the heavens are above the earth, so great is his love for those who fear him; as far as the east is from the west, so far has he removed our transgressions from us.
Psalms 103:8-12

PRAISE

Father, I thank you for your compassion and your gracious ways. For my sins do not receive what they deserve. You abound in love. I am overwhelmed that you are mindful of me, for your love is ever present and comforts me. I am grateful that you are slow to anger, for you LORD, are patient with your children. Father I am glad that you don't accuse, for I know that I have one who accuses me both day and night: Satan is his name. LORD, your love for me is as high as the heavens are above the earth. My heart overflows with joy and my eyes fill with tears of the life given me through you. Merciful you are O LORD, my refuge. Amen.

PROMISE

Then Jesus told them this parable: "Suppose one of you has a hundred sheep and loses one of them. Does he not leave the ninety-nine in the open country and go after the lost sheep until he finds it? And when he finds it, he joyfully puts it on his shoulders and goes home. Then he calls his friends and neighbours together and says, Rejoice with me; I have found

Promises of Forgiveness

my lost sheep. I tell you that in the same way there will be more rejoicing in heaven over one sinner who repents than over ninety-nine righteous persons who do not need to repent."
Luke 15:3-7

PRAISE

Father, I am grateful that you left your flock and glory to come and look for me. I was lost and not sure of my direction in life or the path that I was taking. I was scared because I felt alone, abandoned and betrayed. But you O LORD continued to search my heart and call out to me until I was found. You never gave up on me. My Saviour, you provided me with the light I needed to find my way home. Thank you my Shepherd, for you have reunited me with the flock. Amen.

PROMISE

All the prophets testify about him that everyone who believes in him receives forgiveness of sins through His name.
Acts 10:43

PRAISE

Father, how great it is that if we just believe in you, who you are and what you have done for us with so much love, we will receive the forgiveness of our sins. LORD I believe in you. Thank you for the forgiveness of my sins. Thank you for your word which you gave to the apostles to share. Thank you for the cross and your shed blood, for that is the reason I am washed. Amen.

PROMISE

In him we have redemption through his blood, the forgiveness of sins, in accordance with the riches of God's grace.
Ephesians 1:7

PRAISE

Father I thank you and praise you, for you are my redeemer. Through your Son's blood my sins have been washed away. Your grace and mercy are always before me. Help me to always cast my cares at the foot of the cross. I know, I know, my redeemer lives! Amen.

PROMISE

If we confess our sins, he is faithful and just and will forgive us our sins and purify us from all unrighteousness.
1 John 1:9

PRAISE

Father, I am blessed that you have purified me from all unrighteousness. I was a sinner unworthy of your love, but now I am one who has been saved by grace. You lavish your love upon me. You embrace me with your gentle kindness. You are faithful and just and in you I am/will be perfectly made new. I forgive everyone that has ever wronged me and will remember their sin no more. I too forgive them as you have forgiven me; I release them. All is new, for today is a day that you have made, and I shall rejoice and be glad in it! Amen.

MY CIRCUMSTANCES

Promises of Forgiveness

MY PRAISES

8 Promises of Freedom

Now the LORD is the Spirit, and where the Spirit of the LORD is there is freedom.
2 Corinthians 3:17

Jesus has set us free. Some believers in Christ walk as if they are still in bondage. They live as though they are under the law instead of under grace. Christ died so that we would be set free and move from death to life (1 Corinthians 15:56). He took all of our burdens to the cross with Him so that when we come to the cross to receive Him, we are set free. Free to forgive so we could release the bondage of hurt, grudges and animosity. Free to love so that we could release the bondages of bitterness, division and hatred. Free to prosper so we could release the bondage of poverty. Free to heal so that we could release the bondage of sickness. Free to have peace so we could release the bondage of turmoil and chaos. True freedom in Christ.

We are no longer slaves to sin, and sin is not our master. We do not do as we please in the sinful nature which once was leading us to death, but we have become willing slaves of righteousness and doing what is pleasing to God, who has freed us from the bondage of sin that leads us to eternal life (Romans 6:18).

We must never forget what we have received from Jesus' act of love on the cross. When we decided to take that step of faith and make your good confession, "Jesus is LORD", Lord over us and our life, the chains were broken and the footholds were loosened; we will run and not grow weary (Romans 10:9, Matthew 11:28). It is the LORD that has set us free, and He who sets us free is free indeed.

PROMISE
I run in the path of your commands, for you have set my heart free.
Psalm 119:32

PRAISE
Father I am truly thankful to be free indeed. Your word is truth and has set me free to run down the path that leads to thee. I am grateful, for you have given me the grace to know your word and to be able to run in the path of your commands. For a man who doesn't know or obey your commands has chains around his heart and is not free. But your commands are my keys that have unlocked those chains and you have set my heart and spirit free. Amen.

PROMISE
He upholds the cause of the oppressed and gives food to the hungry. The LORD sets prisoners free.
Psalm 146:7

PRAISE
Father, for many years I have been oppressed by sin,
Made a prisoner and held captive within.

You, Father have rescued me and have broken the lock,
When I am on my knees to you I will talk.

Your word is the food of life and fills me to the brim,
I humbly praise you for bringing me out of sin.

My LORD and my Gatekeeper, who has set me free from the oppressiveness of sin and in my famine state has fed me His word that I may have strength. When the prison doors opened and I was set free, the nourishment you gave me has strengthened me. O LORD my God, my tears have found joy as I run towards my freedom, telling others along the way about my destination and your kingdom. Amen.

PROMISE
Jesus replied, "I tell you the truth, everyone who sins is a slave to sin. Now a slave has no permanent place in the family, but a son belongs to it forever. So if the Son sets you free, you will be free indeed."
John 8:34-36

PRAISE
Father, I am grateful that you share the truth with me,
For it is your truth that has set me free.

Promises of Freedom

I was a slave of sin in times gone by,
You broke those chains so that I could fly.

PROMISE
For we know that our old self was crucified with him, so that the body of sin might be done away with, that we should no longer be slaves to sin.
Romans 6:6

PRAISE
Father, create in me something new,
Something special that brings glory to you.

The old self has passed away,
Manifest your glory through me, for that will stay.

To help me bear fruit and fruit that will last,
The end draws near; I know it comes fast.

I am no longer a slave to sin for I have been set free,
I may fall short but your precious blood covers me.
At the foot of the cross I bow down to thee.

My life is new; my sins had blinded my sight,
Now a slave for Christ, for this I will fight.

Amen.

PROMISE

For sin shall not be your master, because you are not under law, but under grace. When you were slaves to sin, you were free from the control of righteousness. What benefit did you reap at that time from the things you are now ashamed of? Those things result in death! But now that you have been set free from sin and have become slaves to God, the benefit you reap leads to holiness, and the result is eternal life.
Romans 6:14, 20-22

PRAISE

Father, I confess that I once served another master, indulging in the pleasures of the world. Righteousness was not on my mind as long as I filled my fleshly desires. They caused much division in my life and in my household separating me from a relationship with you, for which I was ashamed. Death, pain, torment and suffering were my reward, but now that I serve a new Master, a true living and loving Master. My heart is being renewed daily, strengthened hourly. My mind is becoming renewed and sound through you who strengthens me. My Master, you love me and do not keep me in bondage but have released me into the light that I may taste freedom. My reward is eternal life. Amen.

PROMISE

Now the LORD is the Spirit, and where the Spirit of the LORD is there is freedom.
2 Corinthians 3:17

PRAISE

Father I praise you for I am free,
Because of your Spirit you have given me.
Glory and honour belong to thee.

Amen.

PROMISE

And from Jesus Christ, who is the faithful witness, the firstborn from the dead, and the ruler of the kings of the earth. To him, who loves us and has freed us from our sins by his blood.
Revelation 1:5

PRAISE

Father, I praise your plan to reconcile your children to you. Your love Lord Jesus, your faithfulness and obedience to your Father to your very death has allowed me to be free today. From Adam we were born into death, but through you, LORD the firstborn from the dead, we are born again into life. You have freed me from my sins; in you I am washed. You will never let me fall of that narrow road I carefully tread.

Keep me close, O LORD who is faithful and true,
For on that glorious day I will bow down before you.

For you are the King of kings and LORD of Lords,
Your word till the end will be my sword.

Amen.

MY CIRCUMSTANCES

MY PRAISES

9 PROMISES OF GROWTH

...being confident of this, that he who began a good work in you will carry it on to completion until the day of Christ Jesus

Philippians 1:6

God wants us to grow in love, faith and hope. It's amazing how much growth takes place from the time we are born. Take the gazelle from the animal kingdom: from the time of birth the mother cleans it off, feeds it a little nourishment and encourages it to stand. It stumbles around and falls a few times trying to get its bearings, but it's not too long before it's up and steadily beginning to trot. This process has to occur very quickly, because predators are looking around for something to devour, and they will go after the weak (1 Peter 5:8).

In humans, the baby's first year of life is the fastest year of growth; all other growth takes time. We are fed by our mothers' milk and our physical needs are met by our parents or caregivers. In a matter of weeks we are holding up our head. As time goes on we realize one day that we are able to role from our tummies to our backs without any help. Around the sixth month, we learn to sit up and then crawl, while some have had a couple of teeth already. By then, we now we are no longer just sustained by milk. Puréed fruits and vegetables are being introduced because we are growing up and we require more. Between nine months and the first year, we start to challenge ourselves: climbing furniture and crawling around the table, still holding on of course. Eventually we start taking a few steps before we fall down, but our determination and our God given drive encourages us to get up again. Before we know it, one step in front of the other and we have mastered walking. Gradually our teeth start coming in and we are being prepared for solid food.

Our spiritual life is exactly the same way. When we first accept Jesus Christ, we start off like little children. We may have come in with our baggage, past hurts, bitterness, unforgiveness, hatred and self righteousness, but we're excited at what awaits us and where the LORD will take us in our new journey in Him. We attend church on Sunday for worship, Wednesday for prayer meeting and Friday for Youth group. Women's/men's ministries and other activities often follow. There we are embraced into a group of sons and daughters, our spiritual family in Christ that will help to shepherd you along as a "newborn" member in the body of Christ. These people, along with the rest of the congregation, are our caregivers. They are not going to be perfect, only Christ is. They too like us all are sinners saved by grace yet all striving for one goal: to get to heaven.

In the beginning we require spiritual milk. "Like newborn babes' in Christ, you crave pure spiritual milk, so that by it you may grow up in your salvation, now that you have tasted that the LORD is good" (1 Peter 2:2-3). As we learn more about God and His unconditional love, grace and mercy, God begins to work in our heart. We start changing as we begin to let go of some of those hurts and over time the Spirit within us begins to grow.

This is usually the time when the enemy (Satan) tries to come around looking for someone to devour. To the Christian and especially to the newborns, Satan is our predator. He hates when people give their lives over to Christ because he wants us to remain in our sin doing our own thing, living our own lives separated from God. Satan knows that his time here on earth is short and his fate is already sealed and he will be cast into the lake of fire: "And the devil, who deceived them, was thrown into the lake of burning sulphur, where the beast and the false prophet had been thrown. They will be tormented day and night forever and ever" (Revelation 20:10).

Satan is looking for company. He doesn't care about you; it is your soul he wants. If he can keep you separated from a relationship with Christ, then that is a notch under his belt and he will drag you kicking and screaming with him into the depths of hell. One of Satan's greatest feats was convincing the world that he doesn't exist because if you believed that he exists then you would have to believe that God exist also.

Spiritual growth requires spiritual food and water. Start digging deeper into the intimate things of God through the Bible and prayer and He will reveal more and more of Himself to us. As we continue to grow in

Him and are humbled, our heart begins to soften. We learn how to forgive when we understand how God has forgiven us. That hatred we once had turns to love. Our past hurts are just that, "in the past". We turn in our self-righteousness and put on the righteousness of Christ Jesus. The bitterness in our life will be replaced with a joy that we've never experienced before. Healing takes place as we continue to grow spiritually and are changed from the inside out. We as Christians are called to continue to grow and bear fruit as we strive to become more and more like Christ.

Are you the same person now as you were last year? If not, Amen, to God be the glory. But if you are, then maybe it's time to start searching the deeper things of God. The timing is perfect so don't lose heart, for the growing process continues throughout our life as we obediently follow Jesus, the author and finisher of our faith: "Let us fix our eyes on Jesus, the Author and Perfecter of our faith, who for the joy set before him endured the cross, scorning its shame and sat down at the right hand of the throne of God" (Hebrews 12:2).

PROMISE

The righteous will flourish like a palm tree, they grow like a cedar of Lebanon; they will still bear fruit in old age, they will stay fresh and green.
Psalm 92:12, 14

PRAISE

Father, I praise you for the strength and endurance you give to your children. As you raise us up in you we flourish and do not grow weary or tired, because even in our old age we will bear fruit. To you be the glory and let it be as you say. Amen.

PROMISE

And we, who with unveiled faces all reflect the LORD's glory, are being transformed into his likeness with ever-increasing glory, which comes from the LORD who is the Spirit.
2 Corinthians 3:18

PRAISE

Father, transform me from within and create in me something special and new. Your promises are like sweet incense. I know that you who have started a good work will carry it out until completion. Complete me LORD that I may be like you in every way for your glory. Amen.

THE PROMISE

Then we will no longer be infants, tossed back and forth by the waves, and blown here and there by every wind of teaching and by the cunning and craftiness of men in their deceitful scheming. Instead, speaking the truth in love, we will in all things grow up in to him who is the Head, that is, Christ.
Ephesians 4:14-15

PRAISE

Father, I am grateful that you are raising me up to take solid food that I may stay and remain afloat and swim and not be tossed by the waves. Father, I thank you for providing me with a foundation, that I will not be uprooted with the wind of those whose mouths are cunning, deceitful and scheming. Father, I thank you for a sound mind that I may hear and speak your truth and not be shaken. Grow me up O LORD, for your love is perfect. Never let me go LORD, for your arms are my comfort. Amen.

THE PROMISE

...being confident of this, that he who began a good work in you will carry it on to completion until the day of Christ Jesus.
Philippians 1:6

PRAISE

Father, I am grateful to you for where I am in my life, knowing and being assured that I am being refined and renewed daily. Father, I praise you, for the person I was ten years ago I am not today. The person I was a year ago, I am not today. The person I was three months ago I am not today and the person I was yesterday, I am not today. LORD, you continue to take off the old and put on the new until the day of your coming when I will be completed. To you belongs the glory LORD, the author and finisher of my faith. Amen.

PROMISE

His divine power has given us everything we need for life and godliness through our knowledge of him who called us by his own glory and goodness. Through these he has given us his very great and precious promises, so that through them you may participate in the divine nature and escape the corruption in the world caused by evil desires.
2 Peter 1:3-4

PRAISE

Father, I thank you for equipping me with the armour I need to go against the evil and corruption in the world, the Holy Spirit, which you have left to comfort me and reveal the truth. He shares with me the goodness of your nature and helps me to grow and imitate you through your glory and your mercy. I hang on to the promises which give me hope, knowing that your divine power has given me everything I need for life. Amen.

Promises of Growth

MY CIRCUMSTANCES

Promises of Growth

MY PRAISES

10 Promises of His Presence

...and teaching them to obey everything I have commanded. And surely I am with you always, to the very end of the age.

Matthew 28:20

In Jesus, we're not alone. My heart breaks for those who say that they suffer from loneliness; who feel that they have no one and they are all alone. My prayers go out to them. Some may feel that they are lonely because they don't have a mate or a spouse, but the grass is not always greener on the other side. There are millionaires who have it all: lavish things, well travelled, women or men galore but they are still lonely. There are even people who have been married for 20 or more years and say they still feel alone. The reason they feel this way is because they are separated from a true relationship with God. Let me explain: in Christ there is fullness of joy and God's presence can be felt. The Spirit of Christ is alive and well as He dwells within and everywhere you go He is always with you.

When I was going through my separation with my husband, I felt lonely for a short time until I realized that

I could talk to God. So I would get down on my knees and pray and a peace would come on me and fill my spirit. I would open God's word and promises and know that everything was going to be alright. I also had my friends and family that I would get together and always be in touch with. For the people who are saying, "I don't have any friends" or "My family and I are not in touch so it's not the same thing", my extended church family was instrumental in helping me to stay strong. I began serving my way out of loneliness in different ministries: women's, youth and the missions. God helped to fill that void with fullness of joy once again.

God is faithful all the time. He tells us that He will never leave us nor forsake us. That He will be with us till the very end: "And surely I am with you always, to the very end of the age" (Matthew 28:20). When we are afraid He says, "So do not fear, for I am with you; do not be dismayed, for I am your God. I will strengthen you and help you; I will uphold you with my righteous right hand" (Isaiah 41:10).

God gave Moses the task of rescuing the Jews, Gods' people, out of Egypt from the oppression of the Egyptians. Moses thought this was too extraordinary for him to do, but it wasn't for God. God said to Moses, "'Go. I am sending you to Pharaoh to bring my people the Israelites out of Egypt'. But Moses said to God, 'Who am I that I should go to Pharaoh and bring the Israelites out of Egypt?' And God said, 'I will be with you. And this will be the sign to you that it is I who have sent you'" (Exodus 3:10-12).

There was also the fall of Jericho in (Joshua 6:13-27), when the LORD was with him in battle. Then the LORD said to Joshua, "See, I have delivered Jericho into your hands, along with its king and its' fighting men" (Joshua 6:2).

Loneliness may not be your cross right now. Maybe it is something different, but whatever it is, when we are in battle, whether it be an addiction to drugs or pornography, people against you at work, trouble in your finances, loss of a job or division in your household, God is with us. Some may say, "If God is with us, then why would He allow these things to happen?" Some things God allows for our betterment even though we might not think so at the time (Hebrews 12:11). He will allow these trials to see where you will go for help, if you will rely on yourself or come to Him. We have gotten ourselves into other troubles because of our own disobedience and lack of self control and we need Him to bring us out (James 1:13-14). Whatever the battle, when we persevere in Him, He knows that it will make us stronger.

Don't be afraid. Stand firm in the LORD and in the power of His might and you will see the deliverance the LORD will bring you today. The LORD will fight for you; you need only to be still. In Exodus, Moses answered the people saying; "Do not be afraid. Stand firm and you will see the deliverance the LORD will bring you today. The Egyptians you see today you will never see again. The LORD will fight for you; you need only to be still" (Exodus 14:13-14). Even in the trenches, God is with us and He will see us through it any time, anyplace and anywhere. Either way, there is nothing that we need to worry about or worry over when we have God fighting our battles for us. What a comfort it is to know that He is on our side. Always.

PROMISE
No one will be able to stand up against you all the days of your life. As I was with Moses, so I will be with you; I will never leave you nor forsake you.
Joshua 1:5

PRAISE
Father what a comfort it is, to know that your presence covers me and remains in me always. Wherever I am you will be there also, never to leave me as you live within. I will never be alone in you. Never to forsake me, in you I can depend and my assurance will be victorious in you. Amen.

PROMISE
God is our refuge and strength an ever-present help in trouble. The LORD Almighty is with us; the God of Jacob is our fortress.
Psalm 46:1, 7

PRAISE
Father I thank you for being my refuge and my strength. You have always been there for me in my times of trouble. You provided comfort and love when I felt

abandoned by others. You strengthened me when I was weary. You fill me with joy always and no matter where I am in life, I praise you in my circumstances, for you are with me and the glory is yours. Amen.

PROMISE
For where two or three come together in my name, there am I with them.
Matthew 18:20

PRAISE
Glory to God! How great is it when your favour comes upon us, when we are unified in prayer and even in the small circles, your presence is there. Amen.

PROMISE
...and teaching them to obey everything I have commanded. And surely I am with you always, to the very end of the age.
Matthew 28:20

PRAISE
Father, I am truly grateful to know that you will not leave my side. No matter what I will encounter, as long as I am walking in obedience to your commandments and even in the times that I may falter, you will be with me forever and ever. Amen.

Praise the LORD, for I am grateful that you loved me first and loved me enough to feed me and quench my thirst. When I came to you in all my wickedness and evil ways you received me in and did not turn your back on me. You never drove me away and you always address me as "beloved" and "my child". I come to you and I am not afraid. In your arms I am comforted and there I shall stay. Amen.

PROMISE
For I am convinced that neither death nor life, neither angels nor demons, neither the present nor the future, nor any powers, neither height nor depth, nor anything else in all creation, will be able to separate us from the love of God that is in Christ Jesus our LORD.
Romans 8:38-39

PRAISE
Father, I am thankful that you do not close the doors and channels to you. LORD, you bring me comfort knowing that no matter what I have done or where I have gone, when I come in repentance, your love for me never changes; it will be to you as if I had never left. Your love, LORD, is unconditional, and I am blessed that you allowed my heart to receive it. Amen.

Promises of His Presence

MY CIRCUMSTANCES

MY PRAISES

11 Promises of Joy

Satisfy us in the morning with your unfailing love that we may sing for joy and be glad all our days.

Psalm 90:14

We have joy in Jesus, not in circumstances. In meeting so many people in my circle, one thing that is lacking today is joy. The unemployment is rate rising and marriages and families are feeling the stress of the economic crisis. Parents are having trouble disciplining their children as they get lost in the shuffle, while sinking themselves into debt trying to make ends meet. Suicide among the children is increasing because they are unable to cope with peer pressure, bullying and now "cyber bullying" (through social networks like Facebook), as they struggle with just trying to fit in. Where has the joy gone? Battle after battle and trial after trial. Even among believers, God tells us to "not be surprised at the painful trials you are suffering, as though something strange were happening to you. But rejoice that you participate in the sufferings of Christ, so that you may be overjoyed when his glory is revealed" (1 Peter 4:12). Even as believers, we are not immune to battles and trials, but we know that these trials come for a reason.

In the book of James 1:2-4, he says, "Consider it a pure joy, my brothers whenever you face trials of many kinds, because you know that the testing of your faith develops perseverance. Perseverance must finish its work so that you may be mature and complete, not lacking anything." I am not saying that it is fun to go through these trials and troubles, but in those troubled times, when we believe and trust in God we can be confident because Jesus has overcome the world (John 16:33). So be at peace; it will not harm you. "Thanks be to God, who always leads us in triumphal procession in Christ and through us spreads everywhere the fragrance of the knowledge of Him" (2 Corinthians 2:14).

Our victory and our triumph is guaranteed and assured. We need to give thanks to the LORD even when we don't know what is going on because at the end of that trial there is victory. Things will come but it is in the knowing of what to do and where to go. When we distance ourselves from God in our lives, we are left without hope. But the LORD tells us that in Him there is fullness of joy and the joy of the LORD is our strength (Nehemiah 8:10). When we come to know the LORD in an intimate way, He will restore the joy, change our circumstances and return to us the things that Satan has stolen: happiness, sanity, peace and order.

God works all things for our good. We need to praise Him, in the midst: "And we know that in all things God works for the good of those who love him, who have been called according to his purpose. What, then shall we say in response to this? If God is for us, who can be against us? He who did not spare his own Son, but gave him up for us all—how will he not also, along with him, graciously give us all things?" (Romans 8:28, 31-32). Many are the afflictions of the righteous, but the LORD delivers us out of them all (Psalm 34:19). O, Hallelujah joy!

PROMISE
You have made known to me the path of life; you will fill me with joy in your presence, with eternal pleasures at your right hand.
Psalm 16:11

PRAISE
Father, I am blessed that you loved me enough to make known your path of life. The path that leads to death is much easier to find and so many are on it. You cover and fill me with joy in your presence. This is a path and a place I never want to leave, for your eternal pleasures will endure forever more. Amen.

PROMISE
Satisfy us in the morning with your unfailing love that we may sing for joy and be glad all our days.
Psalm 90:14

PRAISE

Father, when I come to you each morning and fall to my knees, I am comforted. I am in the word searching your truths; my spirit is pleased and made alive. I start my day rejoicing in song, being strengthened every hour for the day is not long. Then tomorrow I will repeat it, and get suited up again, back down on my knees, communing with my Friend. Father, I need my cup to be refilled with all of your ways that I may be glad all of my days. Amen.

PROMISE

If you obey my commands, you will remain in my love, just as I have obeyed my Father's commands and remain in his love. I have told you this so that my joy may be in you and that your joy may be complete.
John 15:10-11

PRAISE

Father, I never want to be outside of your love, for I would perish and wither away.
Give me the faith to obey your commands so in your love I will stay.

For your commands do not bring me harm, but joy, peace and love,
That you so graciously shine down from the heaven's above.

Make me complete, O LORD, from the top of my head to the tip of my toe,

Starting from within so when my joy is complete, it is well with my soul.

Amen.

PROMISE
So with you: Now is your time of grief, but I will see you again, and you will rejoice, and no one will take away your joy.
John 16:22

PRAISE
Blessed be the name of the LORD, for I am grateful for a promise as great as this because I have been grieved for so long, for Satan has run amuck in my life. Yet you, sovereign God, have given me victory over Satan and his schemes and he can't get to me for I am yours. And even though he may try, he will always be defeated. Therefore I will rejoice and I will say again, I will rejoice in a world that is without end, for no one will take away my joy. Amen.

PROMISE
Though you have not seen him, you love him; and even though you do not see him now, you believe in him and are filled with an inexpressible and glorious joy.
1 Peter 1:8

PRAISE
Father, though I have not seen you with my eyes, your presence is felt there is no denying your existence.

You have sent your Word, Jesus, as the example of you manifested in the flesh. For Christ is the radiance of your glory. I love because you loved me first and that is what has filled me with an inexpressible and glorious joy. Amen.

Promises of Joy

MY CIRCUMSTANCES

Promises of Joy

MY PRAISES

12 PROMISES OF LOVE

As the Father has loved me, so have I loved you. Now remain in my love.

John 15:9

God is love. I know that there are different types of love, but it's funny how such a deep and intimate action word such as love is thrown around so loosely these days. We often say things like, "I love those shoes" or "I love that dress" or "I love this car or that tool". Really!? Do we "love" things that can't love us back? or is it more like "I love those shoes" until they start hurting our feet or "I love that tool" until another model comes out.

Even in many relationships people say that they are not happy or they don't feel loved. Things started out great in the beginning when it was new; you know the "puppy love" stage. As the newness wore off the person we found attractive is not as attractive as they once appeared to be. The jokes that made us laugh now annoy us to no end. The praise we once received has now turned into constant criticism. As we look outside our window at the grass, we start to believe that the neighbour's grass looks a lot greener than ours. We all have faults; no one is perfect, but if we could make the choice to love despite the faults, imagine how solid relationships would be today.

There is One whose love is unconditional, unlimited, unmerited, and His love is referred to as "Agapē Love". God's love is perfect, for God is love and it was this type of love that led Him to the cross for you and I (1 John 4:16). God has shown us to what extent He loves us: How many of us would sacrifice our children for others? I would be the first to admit that my hand would definitely struggle to go up, but God so loved the world that He gave His One and only Son to die on the cross for us (John 3:16). Jesus died for us when we were at our most sinful and even enemies towards him, so that we may be reconciled to God (Romans 5:8, Phillipians 3:18, 2 Corinthians 5:18).

Agapē love has supremely to do with the will, not feelings or affections. It is a conquest, a victory and achievement. No one ever naturally loved his enemies. To love one's enemies is a conquest of all our natural inclinations and emotions. This Agapē type of love is in fact the power to love the unlovable, to love people whom we do not like. Imagine that. It is hard to wrap our heads around it, but Jesus died because He loved and He knew that His act of love would pay the price in full for the sins of that generation and generations to come. This would also pave the way for us to have fellowship with Him and share in the eternal life which He came to offer us.

God loves His children and we are His if we claim to have fellowship with Him. He knows that we are not perfect when He calls us, for it is by grace that we are saved. "But because of His great love for us, God, who is rich in mercy, made us alive with Christ even when we were dead in transgression—it is by grace you have been saved" (Ephesians 2:5). It was God who chose to love us first despite our imperfections. "This is how God showed his love among us: He sent His One and only Son into the world that we might live through him. This is love; not that we loved God, but that He loved us and sent his Son as an atoning sacrifice for our sins. We love because He first loved us" (1 John 4:9, 19).

Because we belong to Him, He is patient with us and abounds in love. "The LORD, the LORD, the compassionate and gracious God, is slow to anger, abounding in love and faithfulness" (Exodus 34:6). Sometimes we mess up and sometimes we fall, but He is always there like a loving Father to pick us up. "If we confess our sins, he is faithful and just and will forgive us our sins and purify us from all unrighteousness" (1 John 1:9).

We are God's long-term investment. He paid for us through the blood of Christ. God is faithful and will never give up on us. "If we are faithless, He will remain faithful, for He cannot disown Himself" (2 Timothy 2:13). God's Spirit lives in us because He has given us His Spirit. "We know that we live in Him and He in us, because He has given us of His Spirit" (1 John 4:13). This allows His love for us to overflow to others. "Because God is Love, whoever lives in love lives in God and God in Him" (1 John 4:16). So when we choose to love others as God loves us, we will find relationships, friendships, families and marriages that are everlasting.

PROMISE
Though the mountains be shaken and the hills removed, yet my unfailing love for you will not be shaken nor my covenant of peace be removed says the LORD who has compassion on you.
Isaiah 54:10

PRAISE
Father, I thank you for your unfailing love and the compassion you have shown to me. It's me who is unworthy, but you LORD, tell me otherwise and see me as worthy in your love for me. I am grateful that you are an unchanging God and are not shaken as the mountains and the hills can be. Like a rock, my feet shall be steadily planted in your unfailing love for me and your covenant of peace. Amen.

PROMISE
The LORD appeared to us in the past, saying; "I have loved you with an everlasting love"; I have drawn you with loving-kindness. I will build you up again and you will take up your tambourines and go out to dance with the joyful.
Jeremiah 31:3-4a

PRAISE

Father, I praise you, for you have loved me and continue to love me with your everlasting love. Despite where I have gone astray, you drew me back with loving kindness. Who am I that you are mindful of me? You refer to me as "beloved". Day by day you rebuild what was torn, and I will dance again with my Father in joy and with the joyful. Amen.

PROMISE

And even the very hairs of your head are all numbered. So don't be afraid; you are worth more than many sparrows.
Matthew 10:30-31

PRAISE

Father, I praise your name for blessing me, for I am wonderfully and perfectly made. You have numbered every hair on my head. You have paid attention to detail when it comes to your creation. You have placed me above the animals of the field and the birds of the sky. I will not be afraid for I was made to soar. Amen.

PROMISE

For God so loved the world that He gave his One and only Son, that whoever believes in him shall not perish but have eternal life.
John 3:16

PRAISE

Father, no words that my human lips form, can ever express the gratitude that I feel. The ultimate expression of love on the cross for your children has saved my soul from the fire. Through your Son I have been made clean, washed by His blood. I was once someone who was unworthy and unrighteous, but by you I have been seen as worthy. I have been made righteous through your Son whom I have put my faith and eternal life awaits me. Amen.

PROMISE

As the Father has loved me, so have I loved you. Now remain in my love.
John 15:9

PRAISE

Glory be to God, for I am blessed that you love me and you dwell within me, therefore your love shall remain in me. Keep me, O LORD, is my prayer to you; that I will remain in you. I am on my knees always before thee, leaning not on my own understanding, for you are God and you are love and this request I ask of above. Remain in me, remain in me LORD and I will remain in your love. Amen.

PROMISE

Greater love has no one than this; that he lay down his life for his friends.
John 15:13

PRAISE

LORD, you have called me "friend", for you have revealed the mysteries your Father has shared with you. You loved me to the point of death on the cross. There is none like you LORD, more than just a friend, but a true Saviour, even beyond the end. Amen.

PROMISE

This is how God showed his love among us: He sent his One and Only Son into the world that we might live through him.
1 John 4:9

PRAISE

Father, I thank you and praise you for sending your Son, who is the radiance of your glory. For you showed me who you are through the example of your Sons' life. You empower me through the Holy Spirit you gave me that I may live through Him. I am privileged and honoured, humbled and grateful of the love that you shower upon me. Amen.

Promises of Love

MY CIRCUMSTANCES

Promises of Love

MY PRAISES

13 Promises of Peace

The LORD gives strength to his people; the LORD blesses his people with peace.

Psalm 29:11

True Peace is achievable. In today's age where there is economic instability and unemployment, broken homes, violence and war, suicide and depression, people are stressed and their peace has been stripped away. Marriages in turmoil are common among friends, family, church members and coworkers. People are not sure whether or not they will have a job tomorrow or if they will have their house at the end of the month, because they no longer have an income and the mortgage is due. Yet peace is something God promises: "Peace I leave with you; my peace I give you. I do not give to you as the world gives. Do not let your hearts be troubled and do not be afraid" (John 14:27). God encourages us in these troubled times to not be afraid: "Do not let your hearts be troubled. Trust in God, trust also in me" (John 14:1).

God gives us a genuine peace from within that would quiet even the worst of storms that you could ever encounter. "I have told you these things, so that in me you may have peace. In this world you will have trouble. But take heart! I have overcome the world" (John 16:33). No matter what you're going through right now, God encourages us with His promise of peace: "For a heart at peace gives life to the body" (Proverbs 14:30).

God has a perfect plan for your life. We need not worry because His plan is to prosper us and not to harm us; plans to give us a hope and future: "Then you will call upon me and come and pray to me, and I will listen to you. You will seek me and find me when you seek me with all you heart. I will be found by you, declares the LORD" (Jeremiah 29:11-14).

God and His word alone is our peace. We are even instructed to armour ourselves with His peace. This is something that we are to put on every day (Ephesians 6:14-17). When we accept Jesus as our LORD and personal Saviour, and truly put our trust in Him, No matter what storm or challenge we are currently in, He will work all things out for the good of those who love Him (Romans 8:28). But it may not come in the form or way that you had thought or hoped for. He may even take away things that you have put before Him, but rest assured that He is well able to rebuild and restore it. We just have to be willing to let Him do it His way, then in Him, we can be at peace, sleep in peace, wake up in peace and walk in peace. Just because we may not be able to see Him working or we may feel as if He has forgotten about us, we can be at peace knowing God will never leave us nor forsake us. His best work is done behind the scenes and requires faith. "Now faith is being sure of what we hope for and certain of what we do not see" (Hebrews 11:1). Let me just encourage you with a word from the LORD to put your mind at peace:

> *"For my thoughts are not your thoughts, neither are your ways my ways," declares the LORD "As the heavens are higher than the earth, so are my ways higher than your ways and my thoughts than your thoughts. As the rain and the snow come down from heaven, and do not return to it without watering the earth and making it bud and flourish, so that it yields seed for the sower and bread for the eater, so is my word that goes out from my mouth: it will not return to me empty, but will accomplish what I desire and achieve the purpose for which I sent it. You will go out in joy and be led forth in peace; the mountains and hills will burst into song before you, and all the trees of the field will clap their hands. Instead of the thorn bush will grow the pine tree, and instead of briers the myrtle will grow. This will be for the LORD's renown, for an everlasting sign, which will not be destroyed."*
>
> Isaiah 55:8-13

Be at peace, trust and enter His rest.

PROMISE
The LORD gives strength to his people; the LORD blesses his people with peace.
Psalm 29:11

PRAISE
Blessed be the name of the LORD Jesus Christ, for I give you thanks at all times. In troubled times such as this I will not fret. For you LORD, remain with me and my strength is in you. The world is in a panic but yet you shower me with peace. Some think I live on another planet because I am too calm with what surrounds me: currently separated, division with my daughter, lack of shifts at work, bills coming in, which one to pay first? But I am at peace LORD because I know that you are working on my behalf even though I do not yet see. You are my God, Holy and Precious to me; how much more am I to You? To those that ask, I proudly say I know that my Redeemer lives and I live by His grace. Praise the LORD. Amen.

PROMISE
You will keep in perfect peace, him whose mind is steadfast, because he trusts in you.
Isaiah 26:3

PRAISE
LORD, this scripture brings me not only peace but great joy. I trust in you LORD and believe your words to be true. For it is you and you alone LORD that has shown me nothing but peace and peace of mind, despite

the turmoil of my circumstances. You have placed me outside of them and provided me with peace that can only be found in you. Amen.

THE PROMISE
Peace I leave with you; my peace I give you. I do not give to you as the world gives. Do not let your hearts be troubled and do not be afraid.
John 14:27

PRAISE
Father, your words give me comfort and encouragement, knowing that I need not worry. For you have given and left me with peace that there should be no need for my heart to be weary. The world fears what is before them but I choose to not be troubled or afraid as I once may have been, in a so distant part of my life. To be filled and live in your peace, LORD, is a blessing to dwell in. Amen.

PROMISE
Therefore, since we have been justified through faith, we have peace with God through our LORD Jesus Christ, through whom we have gained access by faith into this grace in which we now stand.
Romans 5:1-2

PRAISE
LORD, I am grateful that I believe in the One you sent with the faith you've given me so that I have peace in you today. It is because of Him that I am able to come

by faith and make my request known to you. Through Jesus, I have access to you which gives me sufficient grace to stand. Amen.

PROMISE
For He himself is our peace, who has made the two one and has destroyed the barrier, the dividing wall of hostility.
Ephesians 2:14

PRAISE
Heavenly Father, I am comforted to know that you're my peace in which my feet have been fitted in. You LORD, are One, dwelling in the heavens and coming down to earth, walking among us destroying the barriers and the high places while setting us straight. LORD, you are forever providing us with love and hope, separating the sheep and the goats and dividing the walls of hostility. Amen.

PROMISE
Now the LORD of peace Himself, give you peace at all times and in every way. The LORD be with all of you.
2 Thessalonians 3:16

PRAISE
LORD, you have filled my spirit with so much peace that even in and through my circumstances I understood why I wasn't in despair. My trust in you and your promises are what have assured me that you will always be with me to the very end of the age. Amen.

MY CIRCUMSTANCES

MY PRAISES

14 Promises of Salavation

For it is by grace you have been saved, through faith—
and this not from yourselves, it is the gift of God.
Ephesians 2:8

Salvation is not something that can be purchased or gained by good deeds or works. Salvation is a free gift offered by God. It does not cost us anything because Jesus has paid the price for our salvation through the cross by which He died for us.

He paid for us with His blood so that we could be saved and reconciled to the Father who is in heaven. We are born with a sin nature and that sin separates us from God (Isaiah 59:2). If we die without accepting Jesus as our Saviour or having repented of our sins and turning from our wicked and evil ways, we end up in hell and torment burning in the lake of fire. But when we do accept Jesus Christ as our personal LORD and Saviour, we allow the saving grace of Jesus to come into our lives. Jesus did not come to condemn the world but to save the world through Him (John 3:17). God's whole purpose in sending His Son was to save the world, that whoever believes in Him shall not perish but have eternal life (John 3:16). It is more than just believing in Him, it is asking Him to save us and receive the gift that He has come to offer us (James 2:19).

Some people have said to me, "Well I don't think a loving God would send people to hell", and I tell them, "You are right, a loving God doesn't send people to hell, He is patient with us. Hell was never created for people, but when you reject Christ you have chosen to go there". Then I show them 2 Peter 3:9: "The LORD is not slow in keeping his promise, as some understand slowness. He is patient with you, not wanting anyone to perish, but everyone to come to repentance". Matthew 25:41 says, "Then he will say to those on his left, Depart from me, you who are cursed, into the eternal fire prepared for the devil and his angels." So because Jesus came to save, when we reject your Saviour, we stand condemned. Most people know and can even recite John 3:16, but do not understand how serious its' meaning is. "For God so loved the world that He gave His One and Only Son, that whoever believes in him shall not perish but have eternal life." But they do not know or understand the rest of the scripture and how serious it is: "For God did not send His Son into the world to condemn the world but to save the world through Him. Whoever believes in Him is not condemned, but whoever does not believe stands condemned already because he has not believed in the name of God's One and Only Son" (Vs. 17-18).

Salvation is extended to all: Jew, Gentile, Muslim, Hindu, etc. Christ died for sins once for all, the righteous for the unrighteous, to bring us to God (1 Peter

3:18). For the Jew, it is Christ that died for you. For the Muslim, it is Christ that died for you. For the Hindu, it is Christ that died for you. For the Gentiles, it is Christ that died for you. For the Scientologists, it is Christ that died for you, once for all.

> *Anyone who trusts in him will never be put to shame. For there is no difference between Jew and Gentile—the same LORD is LORD of all and richly blesses all who call on him, for "Everyone who calls on the name of the LORD will be saved." How, then, can they call on the one they have not believed in? And how can they believe in the One of whom they have not heard? And how can they hear without someone preaching to them? And how can they preach unless they are sent? As it is written "How beautiful are the feet of those who bring good news!" But not all the Israelites accepted the good news. For Isaiah says, "LORD, who has believed our message?" Consequently faith comes from hearing the message, and the message is heard through the word of Christ. But I ask: Did they not hear? Of course they did: Their voice has gone out into all the earth, their words to the ends to ends of the world.*
> Romans 10:11-18

God doesn't want one person to perish (1 Timothy 2:4). He wants all to come to repentance that they may see that the LORD is good, and that we may be made alive in Christ:

Promises of Salvation

As for you, you were dead in your transgressions and sins, in which you used to live when you followed the ways of this world and of the ruler of the kingdom of the air, the spirit who is now at work in those who are disobedient (that disobedient spirit is Satan). All of us also lived among them at one time, gratifying the cravings of our sinful nature and following its desires and thoughts. Like the rest, we were by nature objects of wrath. But because of his great love for us, God, who is rich in mercy, made us alive with Christ even when we were dead in transgressions – it is by grace you have been saved. And God raised us up with Christ and seated us with him in the heavenly realms in Christ Jesus, in order that in the coming ages He might show the incomparable riches of his grace, expressed in his kindness to us in Christ Jesus. For it is by grace you have been saved, through faith-- and this not from yourselves, it is the gift of God-- not by works, so that no one can boast. For we are God's workmanship, created in Christ Jesus to do good works, which God prepared in advance for us to do.
Ephesians 2:1-10

But encourage one another daily, as long as it is called "Today"', so that none of you may be hardened by sin's deceitfulness; so "Today, if you hear his voice, do not harden your hearts.
Hebrews 3:13, 15

Choose Christ today and accept His gift, for "Salvations found in no one else, for there is no other name under heaven given to men by which we must be saved" (Acts 4:12).

If you would like to accept Jesus' free gift of salvation and ask Him to save you, making Him your LORD and personal Saviour, then say this prayer:

> "LORD Jesus, Son of God and Saviour of the world, you died on the cross for me, that I may have life. You bore the punishment on the cross that I should have endured because of your love for me. I believe you died for my sins and rose again; and today Jesus, as long as it is called today, I declare that I am a sinner and ask you come into my heart and cleanse me of my sins. Save me, O LORD, from the schemes of the evil one, for I do not want my resting place to be in hell with him, but I want to be in the holy places of heaven where you dwell. Wash me and make me new, guide me and make my path straight, protecting me as I take this step with you. Cover me with the blood of Christ Jesus. I thank you, LORD, for receiving me and hearing my prayer from this day forward. In Jesus' name I pray. Amen."

If you have just prayed that prayer and were sincere about what you have asked Christ to do for you, my brothers and sisters you are saved. Prepare for the LORD to move in your life and life as you know it will never be the same. Glory be to the Most High God.

PROMISE

The salvation of the righteous comes from the LORD; he is their stronghold in time of trouble. The LORD helps them and delivers them; he delivers them from the wicked and saves them, because they take refuge in him.
Psalm 37:39-40

PRAISE

Father, I thank you for you are my salvation that has provided me with freedom: freedom from sin and the strongholds of the evil one.
My breakthrough has come and "Hallelujah!" is sung.

On the cross, you boar my shame and you took my punishment and my pain.

LORD you are my rock and my refuge and my salvation is secured in you. Amen.

PROMISE

In that day they will say, "Surely this is our God; we trusted in him, and he saved us. This is the LORD we trusted in him; let us rejoice and be glad in his salvation.
Isaiah 25:9

PRAISE

Father, you are my God and I will trust in you for you have saved me because I have trusted in you. You have made my joy complete. I shall rejoice and be glad in my salvation for you have redeemed me to you, claiming me as your own. No one can take that away from me because surely you are my God. Amen.

PROMISE
She will give birth to a Son, and you are to give him the name Jesus, because he will save his people from their sins.
Matthew 1:21

PRAISE
Father, I praise you and I thank you for sending your Son, who is the salvation of the world. For you, LORD, became flesh that you would live among us so that we would be saved. I am grateful of the magnitude of love you have for me and saving me from my sins so that I will one day dwell with you. Amen.

PROMISE
They replied, "Believe in the LORD Jesus, and you will be saved—you and your household.
Acts 16:31

PRAISE
LORD, I believe in you and you have saved me. I have taught my daughter Shawntelle about you. I hang on to your promises and continue to pray. Yet, I want Satan to know that I am waiting and expecting you to show up. He will be defeated and Shawntelle shall be saved and reconciled to you and will be spared from what is to come. Save her LORD, and turn her towards your glorious light. She is saved. She is saved. Hallelujah, thank you for my household. Amen.

PROMISE
For it is by grace you have been saved, through faith — and this not from yourselves, it is the gift of God.
Ephesians 2:8

PRAISE
Glory be to God, for what a loving gift you have given me, that your grace is sufficient to allow me to be saved. I know there was nothing I have done to contribute to it, nor nothing I could have said to grant me this. But through your grace, I do humbly embrace the gift of life eternal given me through faith in you. For your shed blood has atoned for me on the cross. Amen.

PROMISE
Therefore he is able to save completely those who come to God through him, because he always lives to intercede for them.
Hebrews 7:25

PRAISE
Father, I thank you for sending the One who intercedes for me on my behalf. One who came and showed me the way to you. One who saved me by the shedding of His blood. One who was raised from the dead, showing me life eternal. One who reconciled me to my great Love from above, the precious One named Jesus. Amen.

MY CIRCUMSTANCES

Promises of Salvation

MY PRAISES

15 Promises of Strength

He will keep you strong to the end, so that you will be blameless on the day of our LORD Jesus Christ.
1 Corinthians 1:8

Strength and courage aren't always measured in medallions and victories but they are measured in the struggles that we have overcome. "The strongest people aren't always the people who win, but the people who don't give up when they lose" (Ashley Hodgeson).

We can depend on God as our source of strength. He gives strength to the weary and increases the power of the weak. Even our youth at times grow weary and tired and our young men will stumble and fall, but it is those whose hope is in the LORD that will renew their strength. Throughout the Bible, God shows us many scriptures of this promise where we can tap in to.

Sometimes even just to get out of bed, we need to draw from the LORD's strength. Many of us who are parents at times feel that we are at our wits end when it comes to our children, even though we love them with all our hearts; this is when we have to tap in to the LORD's strength; for that is what will sustain us.

Promises of Strength

People who have been oppressed for years as children, or adults whether they be slave or free in any country, are sustained from day to day by God's strength, not from the strength of their own. "God is our refuge and strength, an ever-present help in trouble" (Psalm 46:1).

These are some inspirational quotes from famous people within a Godly perspective:

You gain strength, courage and confidence by every experience in which you really stop to look fear in the face. You are able to say to yourself, "I have lived through this horror. I can take the things that come along. You must do the things you think you cannot do.
Eleanor Roosevelt

Some people believe that holding on and hanging in there are signs of great strength. However, there are times when it takes much more strength to know when to let go -- and then do it.
Ann Landers

Faith is the strength by which a shattered world shall emerge into the light.
Helen Keller

And some more from the Bible:

So do not fear, for I am with you; do not be dismayed, for I am your God. I will strengthen you and help you. I will uphold you with my righteous right hand.
Isaiah 41:10

The LORD is my light and my salvation, whom shall I fear? The LORD is the stronghold of my life of whom shall I be afraid?
Psalm 27:1

The salvation of the righteous comes from the LORD; he is their stronghold in time of trouble. The LORD helps them and delivers them; he delivers them from the wicked and saves them, because they take refuge in him.
Psalm 37:39-40

So no matter what you are facing, or whatever challenge, trial or test you may be encountering; remember God's promise of strength and draw from Him. Never forget to tell yourselves "I can do everything through Christ who gives me strength."
Philippians 4:13

PROMISE
Whom have I in heaven but you? And earth has nothing I desire besides you. My flesh and my heart may fail, but God is the strength of my heart and my portion forever.
Psalm 73:25-26

PRAISE

Father, no matter what is going on in my life, whether it is something good or bad, you are all I need. On earth there is no one that can compare to you. Like David, my flesh and my heart may fail, but it cannot separate me from your love. Sweet LORD my God, you are my strength and full portion for my spirit forever. Amen.

PROMISE

He gives strength to the weary and increases the power to the weak. But those who hope in the LORD will renew their strength. They will soar on wings like eagles; they will run and not grow weary, they will walk and not be faint.
Isaiah 40:29, 31

PRAISE

Father, these are powerful and encouraging words you have left me with. When I was weary, LORD, you strengthened me each day with your grace to sustain me. I am no longer weak, for it is time for me to fly on wings like eagles and you, O LORD, will be there to catch me if I need help. My hope is in you all day long. In troubled times my heart will not be troubled; my rock and my refuge, my God. Amen.

PROMISE

He will keep you strong to the end, so that you will be blameless on the day of our LORD Jesus Christ.
1 Corinthians 1:8

PRAISE

Father, I am forever grateful that your strength will keep me strong until the end, for my flesh would never be able to endure. But you who are Spirit will allow the spirit that dwells inside of me to endure. Praise and glory belong to you LORD, for you see me as blameless because of your one and only Son. Amen.

PROMISE

Now to him who is able to do immeasurably more than all we ask or imagine, according to his power that is at work within us,
Ephesians 3:20

PRAISE

Father, I praise you, for you LORD can do all things. You give me strength to go above and beyond what the world may see as impossible or difficult. But you, LORD, are able to do immeasurably more than all I can ask or imagine. When I submit and let your power work within me, I am capable of doing all things in you. Amen.

PROMISE

But the LORD is faithful, and he will strengthen and protect you from the evil one.
2 Thessalonians 3:3

PRAISE

LORD, I am blessed, for you are a faithful God. Even when there are times when my faith may fail, you never change. You strengthen me when I am weak, because you are faithful. You protect me from the evil one and all his schemes. You cover me and shield me faithfully and you will remain faithful to me in love until the very end of the age. Satan has no hold over me for I am yours. Amen.

PROMISE

And the God of all grace, who called you to his eternal glory in Christ, after you have suffered a little while, will himself restore you and make you strong, firm and steadfast.
1 Peter 5:10

PRAISE

Father, you truly are a God who is full of grace, that you have allowed me time to come to know the eternal glory in Christ my Saviour. I praise you in my suffering O LORD, for I know that you went through it with me and that is what made it easier for me to bear. I am now well on my way to restoration in you. You have given me and continue to give me strength, as I walk firmly in the path which you have set before me. This is my story. Amen.

Promises of Strength

MY CIRCUMSTANCES

Promises of Strength

MY PRAISES

16 Promises of the Holy Spirit

And if the Spirit of him who raised Jesus from the dead is living in you, he who raised Christ from the dead will also give life to your mortal bodies through his Spirit, who lives in you.

Romans 8:11

The apostle Peter speaks to the crowd, and this applies to us today. "Repent and be baptized, every one of you, in the name of Jesus Christ for the forgiveness of your sins. And you will receive the gift of the Holy Spirit. The promise is for you and your children and for all who are far off—for all whom the Lord our God will call" (Acts 2:38-39). "Those who accepted his message were baptized, and about three thousand were added to their number that day" (Acts 2:41).

Jesus made a promise to his disciples, before he left to go back to heaven and we too who are believers and follow Him are also his disciples. In John 16:7, 13-14, Jesus said, "I tell you the truth; it is for your good that I am going away. Unless I go away, the Counsellor will not come to you; but if I go, I will send him to you...But when he, the Spirit of truth, comes, he will guide you into all truth. He will not speak on his own; he will speak only what he hears, and he will tell you what is yet to come. He will bring glory to me by taking from what is mine and making it known to you." Yes, He (the Spirit is masculine) will give us the inside scoop about the hidden things of God, for our eyes shall be opened.

I remember before I came to know the LORD that when I would read the Bible I would understand somewhat of what I was reading, but it only seemed to penetrate the surface. But when I gave my heart to the LORD and was baptized, the word became a daily part of my life. I would pray to God to give me a deeper understanding to His word and it was amazing because I started to get revelations out of what I was reading. This never could have come without the knowledge from the Spirit. Why wouldn't it come to me before, but did now? The Spirit reveals the deeper things of God and opens up our understanding of Him, because now the relationship between us and the Creator has been reconciled.

Jesus Promises the Holy Spirit. "If you love me, you will obey what I command. And I will ask the Father, and He will give you another Counsellor to be with you forever—the Spirit of truth. The world cannot accept him, because it neither sees him nor knows him. But you know him, for he lives with you and will be in you. I will not leave you as orphans; I will come to you" (John 14:15-18). "If any one loves me he will obey my teaching. My Father will love him, and we will come to him and make our home with him. He who does not love me will not obey my teaching. These words you hear are not my own, they belong to the Father who sent me. All this I have spoken while still with you. But the Counsellor, the Holy Spirit, whom the Father will send in my name, will teach you all things and will remind you of everything I have said to you" (John 14:23-26).

Repent and be baptized. When we have repented of our sins and put our faith in Jesus (as I wrote about in the last chapter), we should then be fully baptized in water (fully submerged). In this we symbolically participate in the death, burial and resurrection of our Lord Jesus Christ. It is a public confession that we have died to self and are raised and made alive in Christ Jesus (Romans 6:3-4, Colossians 2:9, 1 Timothy 6:12). Baptism alone does not save us; faith in Jesus Christ does. Some people say, "Well, I was baptized as a baby". Perhaps you were dedicated to God by your parent's through sprinkling of water or making a cross with oil on the forehead, but the bible does not say that we are buried with Christ by doing this. Only full submersion of the body from head to toe can.

Children don't need to be baptized because the kingdom of heaven is made for them. In Luke 18:15-17, the Bible tells us that people were also bringing babies and children to Jesus to have him touch them. When the disciples saw this, they rebuked them. But Jesus called the children to him and said, "Let the little children come to me, and do not hinder them, for the kingdom of God belongs to such as these. I tell you the truth, anyone who will not receive the kingdom of God like a little child will never enter it." Children and babies are too young to make the decision of what it really means to be a follower of Christ and distinguish between right and wrong, that's why when the rapture happens, *all* of the children will be gone. "How dreadful it will be in those days for pregnant women and nursing mothers!" (Matthew 24:19). Seek comfort in the LORD your God.

When we have a life that is through the Spirit, there is no more condemnation from sin. I am not saying that this is now a license to sin it up without any consequence. What I am saying is now that we have been born again we no longer strive or desire what is pleasing to ourselves, but what is pleasing to God. For all have sinned and fall short of the glory of God (Romans 3:23). So when we do sin we are covered by Jesus' blood - it will be as if we never sinned at all. That's why I said that heaven will be full of former sinners, but sinners who have been saved by grace through faith in Jesus Christ.

> *There is now no condemnation for those who are in Christ Jesus, because through Christ Jesus the law of the Spirit of life set me free from the law of sin and death. For what the law was powerless to do in that it was weakened by the sinful nature, God did, by sending his own Son in the likeness of sinful man to be a sin offering. And so he condemned sin in sinful man, in order that the righteous requirements of the law might be fully met in us, who do not live according to the sinful nature but according to the Spirit. Those who live*

according to the sinful nature have their minds set on what that nature desires; but those who live in accordance with the Spirit have their minds set on what the Spirit desires. The mind of sinful man is death, but the mind controlled by the Spirit is life and peace, the sinful mind is hostile towards God. It does not submit to God's law, nor can it do so. Those controlled by the sinful nature cannot please God.

You, however, (who believe and are baptized into Christ) are controlled not by the sinful nature but by the Spirit, if the Spirit of God lives in you. And if anyone does not have the Spirit of Christ, he does not belong to Christ. But if Christ is in you, your body (the flesh) is dead because of sin, yet your spirit is alive because of righteousness (Christ). And if the Spirit of him who raised Jesus from the dead is living in you, he who raised Christ from the dead will also give life to your mortal bodies through his Spirit, who lives in you.
Romans 8:1-11

The Spirit intercedes on our behalf.

In the same way, the Spirit helps us in our weakness. We do not know what we ought to pray for, but the Spirit himself intercedes for us with groans that words cannot express. And He who searches our hearts knows the mind of the Spirit, because the Spirit intercedes for the saints in accordance with God's will
Romans 8:26-27

Promises of the Holy Spirit

The book of Acts has many accounts of the Holy Spirit working through the lives of Jesus' disciples: it shows us how He warned the disciples of impending danger (Acts 21:11-14) and hindered them from entering in certain towns and cities (Acts 16:6-8) and instructed them on which roads to travel and where they should go (Acts 8:26-31). The Spirit allowed them to heal the sick (Acts 5:12-16), make the crippled walk (Acts 14:8-10), cast out demons (Acts 8:6-7) and bring back people from the dead (Acts 9:36-41). This powerful Holy Spirit given to the apostles is the same Spirit given to us today. The LORD tells us that we will do even greater things than these (John 14:12-14). When we choose to live in the Spirit and not by the flesh, we are able to do great things for the glory of the Kingdom of God, such as laying hands on people and having them be healed from cancers and blindness, joint pains and other ailments, so that God will receive the glory. We can prophesy into peoples' lives and see the manifestation of that prophesy come to fruition as they are delivered from addictions and receive peace and breakthroughs in hard circumstances as they praise the LORD.

PROMISE

Even on my servants, both men and women, I will pour out my Spirit in those days.
Joel 2:29

PRAISE

Father, what a blessing it is to be a servant of the Most High God; to receive the pouring out of your Spirit in these days. Your Spirit which brings life, power and love will strengthen and comfort me. LORD, I thank you for the Spirit that dwells within me today as I am able to do great things with you and through you, for something as great as having a powerful ministry that will impact millions can only be possible in you. Give me the grace to receive and manifest the gifts of prophesy and visions you have for me. Amen.

PROMISE
If you then, though you are evil, know how to give good gifs to your children, how much more will your Father in heaven give the Holy Spirit to those who ask him!
Luke 11:13

PRAISE
Father, despite our wickedness at times, you died for us when we were at our worst. Despite our faithlessness at times, you always remain faithful to us. Father though we are evil, you loved us and still love us today, not giving up on us and hoping that we may come to repentance and receive the goodness that you have for us. In your grace and in your mercy you have poured out the gift of the Holy Spirit. Who am I, that you are so loving and mindful? All I need to do is ask my Creator, who tells me that I am wonderfully and perfectly made. Amen.

PROMISE
And I will ask the Father, and he will give you another Counsellor to be with you forever—the Spirit of truth. The

world cannot accept him, because it neither sees him nor knows him. But you know him, for he lives with you and will be in you.
John 14:16-17

PRAISE

Father, I am forever grateful that you have left me a Counsellor and a Comforter who will teach me truths about you. One who knows your nature and will intercede for me on my behalf. When I know not what to pray, I will not be discouraged or despaired for the Spirit will know what to pray for. You have sent me one that will teach and reveal the mysteries of you. You have left me equipped, protected and reassured. Glory be to the Most High God. Amen.

PROMISE

Peter replied, "Repent and be baptized, every one of you, in the name of Jesus Christ for the forgiveness of your sins. And you will receive the gift of the Holy Spirit."
Acts 2:38

PRAISE

Father, I give you praise, I give you glory and I give you honour and thanks, for you alone are worthy for giving me a gift as great as this. My sins have been forgiven through the blood of your One and only Son and your Spirit has been planted in me to start a fresh and new. As a symbol of my gratitude and worship of you, I have publically declared before people that you are my LORD and I am baptized into your death, burial and resurrection. And as you have promised LORD, my life will never be the same, because of your shed blood. It was given to me freely, but cost your Son dearly. This is His act of Love to the full. Amen.

PROMISE

And if the Spirit of him who raised Jesus from the dead is living in you, he who raised Christ from the dead will also give life to your mortal bodies through his Spirit, who lives in you.
Romans 8:11

PRAISE

I sing hallelujah to you LORD, for I am no longer dead in my transgressions. You have given me eternal life and have brought me back from the dead in spirit. You have given me a new life in this mortal body and now if I were to die I will become immortal through your Spirit. You have given me a new life and a new outlook, for I now see with spiritual eyes the things I've never seen with mortal eyes. Everything has become new. I will fulfill my purpose and I will be capable of all things, for you are with me and in me. Give me the strength LORD to decrease that you may continue to increase. I will fight the good fight and finish the race until I am called home, for when I am absent from the body, I will be present with my LORD. Amen.

Promises of the Holy Spirit

MY CIRCUMSTANCES

MY PRAISES

17 Closing

I hope that this book will be a reflection of what God has done through me for the glory of His Kingdom, as He allowed me to put aside the fears and the doubts and the other insecurities I once had and step out in faith.

I look forward to meeting all who have read this book and hearing your testimonies about how the LORD has impacted your lives. If it is not here, then in heaven. I have asked the LORD if I would be able to meet those who were impacted by the book and who came to know Him before the rapture and after the rapture in heaven because I know that it would be impossible to meet everyone in the time allotted to us here on earth.

Don't just read this book one time. Read through it often, carry it with you, share it with your friends or get them a copy so that they can have it with them as well. The times ahead will be hard as we have entered into a new age, but you don't have to go through them alone. For those who are already in the body of Christ I hope that this book gave you some encouragement and renewed your mind and your strength. Keep on pressing on and fight the good fight. For those who have said the

Closing

prayer and have made this life changing decision, I pray that there is a baptizing, Bible teaching and Spirit-filled church in your area.

If you have chosen not to follow Him, then I pray that the LORD will bring you to the grace of repentance and lead you to the knowledge of the truth and continue to protect you, and convict your heart. As long as you still have breath there is hope, but you are playing with fire. I also pray that you hang on to this book as a guide for when the rapture happens, but first and foremost, get yourself a Bible before they become outlawed, because you may be required at that time to lead someone to the truth now that your eyes have been opened. Amen.

It hasn't always been easy but well worth the wait, because God never disappoints. The relationship with my daughter has improved a thousand fold. I praise the LORD every day for bringing her to salvation, for He is good. We both admit that we're not perfect, but we strive to love one another just the same as Christ loves us; unconditionally. I also know that she is in good hands now, so I need not worry, though I continue to pray for her daily. I pray that she too will hang on to God's promises and what He has in store for her life.

I love you Shawntelle with all my heart. I am so proud of where you've come from and where the LORD will take you!
Mom

There are still the promises that have not yet come to pass. I say "yet" because I am still expecting God to show up, that's why I reflect on His promises daily. I am

Closing

still waiting in His perfect timing with patience, joy, strength, peace, love and great expectation. Nothing can compare to the one that has already come to pass. My daughter Shawntelle coming to church and turning her life around, and deciding for herself that she wants to give her heart unto the LORD. I don't think anything in this world can compare to a soul that is saved for the Kingdom of God.

I really hope that you have made a choice by the end of this book to give your life to God. If you have already made the choice, tell others how they too can be saved and share in the promise of eternal life. I hope that this book has given you the faith to hang on to God's promises, what He has and will do.

If you are ever visiting Canada and you are coming to the Toronto, Ontario area, make sure you stop by and fellowship with us at:
Faith Miracle Temple
280 Yorkland Boulevard
Toronto, Ontario, Canada, M2J 1R5.

www.fmttoronto.ca
Tel: 416-650-9550

The Senior Pastor is Bishop Dr Al Baxter B.Sc D.D. and the Associate Pastor Rev. Mark Anthony Baxter B. Th. So, until then, fellow saints, may the LORD bless you and keep you; may the LORD make His face to shine upon you and be gracious to you; may the LORD turn His face toward you and give you peace. Amen.

Closing

18 OTHER PROMISES

Afraid—Psalm 4:8; Psalm 23:4; Isaiah 35:4; Romans 8:3739; 2 Corinthians 1:10;2 Timothy 1:7; Hebrews 13:6

Anxious—Psalm 55:22; Isaiah41:13; Matthew 6:25; Matthew 11:28-29; Philippians 4:6-7; 1 Peter 5:7

Confused—Psalm 32:8; Isaiah 42:16; John 8:12; John 14:27; 1 Corinthians 2:15-16; James 1:5

Despair—Psalm 119:116; Isaiah 57:15; Jeremiah 32:17; Hebrews 10:35

Depressed—Deuteronomy 3:18; Psalm 34:18; Isaiah 49:13-15; Romans 5:5

Disappointed—Psalm 22:4-5; Isaiah 49:23; Matthew 19:25-26; Mark 9:21-24; John 15:7; Ephesians 3:20

Doubt—Psalm 34:22; John 3:18; John 11:25-26; Romans 4:5; 1 John 4:15-16

Filled with Longing—Psalm 37:4; Psalm 84:11; Psalm 103:5; Luke 12:29-31

Failure—Joshua 1:9; Romans 3:23-24; Romans 5:8; Hebrews 10:36; 1 John 1:8-9

Other Promises

Grief—Psalm 119:50; Psalm 119:76-77; Jeremiah 31:13; Matthew 5:4; John 16:20-22; 1 Thessalonians 4:13; Revelation 21:3-4

Guilt—2 Samuel 14:14; Psalm 130:3-4; Romans 8:1-2; 1 Corinthians 6:11; Ephesians 3:12; Hebrews 10:22-23

In Need—Isaiah 58:11; John 6:35; 2 Corinthians 9:10-11; Ephesians 3:20-21; Philippians 4:19

Patience—Psalm 27:13-14; Psalm 37:7,9; Romans 2:7; 1 Timothy 1:16; Hebrews 6:12; 1 Peter 3:9

Persecution—Genesis 50:20; Psalm 37:1-2; Matthew 5:10-12; 2 Corinthians 4:8-12; 2 Timothy 1:11-12; 1 Peter 3:13-14

Obedience—Exodus 14:23; Matthew 16:27; John 8:31-32; John 14:21,23; James 1:25

Sickness—Psalm 23:4; Psalm 73:26; Isaiah 57:18; Matthew 8:16-17; John 16:33; Romans 8:37-39; James 5:14-15

Suffering—Psalm 34:19; Nahum 1:7; John 16:33; Romans 8:16-17; 1 Peter 2:20-21; 1 Peter 4-12-13

Temptation—Job 23:10-11; 1 Corinthians 10:13; Hebrews 2:18; Hebrews 4:15-16; James 1:2-4; James 1:13-14; 1 Peter 5:8-10

Weakness—Psalm 72:13; Isaiah 41:10; Romans 8:26; 1 Corinthians 1:7-9; 2 Corinthians 4:7-9 and 12:9-10

19 THE ROMANS ROAD TO SALVATION

There's a simple way to show somebody how to be saved using the Bible. If you already know the LORD and want to share the good news with others but don't know how, here's an easy way. Our church wanted to reach souls for Jesus but like most people, some of us just didn't know where to begin or what to say without confusing and losing people along the way. We had what is called, a witness training school. A pastor named Gene Pritchard, from Grace Bible Church of Central Florida, Orlando came up to our church to teach the classes every day for about five days. Gene said to photocopy the handouts given out which I used in this section so feel free, and teach other brothers and sisters in other churches, so that's what I've been doing as I also share it with you.

To God be the glory; great things He has done. Some will come to salvation, but sadly many will reject the word (Matthew 7:13). It is not you they are rejecting but Jesus (John 15:20). God has already prepared the hearts ahead of time to receive the word (Acts 16:14). Always pray before going and along your travels, asking God to bring those hearts to you, setting up divine appointments. You will be surprised how things just unfold.

I hope that this will be as helpful for you as it was for me and our church. We have already begun to see God working in a powerful way in the real life training sessions: Two members of the Florida training team, another church member and myself went to share the gospel at a townhouse complex. One Muslim father of three daughters was so glad to hear about Jesus. He was made to feel guilty and condemned by his fellow community unless he did his religious duties of praying five times a day, etc. When we lead him down the Romans Road, he quickly grasped to the loving and forgiving Jesus, accepting him on the spot. With tears in his eyes as he finished the prayer, he said that a peace come over him. Right after he accepted Jesus, he called his three daughters downstairs and said to them, "Now you girls listen to what these two ladies have to say", and listen intently they did. They too gave their hearts to the LORD that very same day. God is good.

Just meeting people on the street, talking to them and seeing and hearing the despair, some never heard about this Jesus or knew about salvation, and after going over the Romans Road with them, they were eager for change and a new hope. Many attend the church today and are sharing with others how they can be saved.

It's not about converting people to a religion or to our church; it's about salvation and a new life through a relationship with Jesus. If there is a Bible believing church near them, encourage them to go. If they don't have a church to go to, then offer to pick them up or extend an invitation to your own church.

The Romans Road to Salvation Study Guide

(I) We can know that we are saved (1 John 5:13). There are three things a person must know and do to be saved:

1. *A sinner must know that salvation is NEEDED:*
   a. Because all have sinned (Romans 3:10; 3:23).
   b. Because unforgiven sin brings spiritual death (Romans 5:12; 6:23).

2. *A sinner must know that salvation has been PROVIDED:*
   God loves us, even as sinners and sent His Son, Jesus, to die for our sins. We can be forgiven of <u>all</u> our sins and be reconciled to God through faith in His Son (Romans 5:8)!

3. *A sinner must ACCEPT the salvation God has provided:*
   Salvation is received by faith and prayer (Romans 10:9-13).

We will now make a "Road Map" in your Bible so that you won't have to memorize the scripture references; they will be written in so you will know exactly where to turn next. Use the following scriptures:

a. *1 John 5:13*...next to this scripture write Rom 3:10. Then turn to Romans 3:10.
b. *Romans 3:10*...beside this scripture write 3:23. Go to:
c. *Romans 3:23*...beside this scripture write 5:12. Go to:
d. *Romans 5:12*...beside this scripture write 6:23. Go to:
e. *Romans 6:23*...beside this scripture write 5:8. Go to:
f. *Romans 5:8*...beside this scripture write 10: 9-13. Go to:
g. *Romans 10: 9-13*...that's it!

(II) **To help people see their need to be saved, ask two questions (Write them somewhere in the front of your Bible to remind you):**

1. If you should die today, are you 100% certain that you would go to heaven?
2. If you should die today and stand before God and He asked you why He should let you in heaven, what would you say?

The purpose of these questions is not to judge or condemn the person's beliefs, but to assess where they are spiritually. We are merely being humble and listening; God has given us ears for a reason. What we are trying to understand is if their faith is truly in Jesus, themselves something else or nothing at all. You will find that most people think they are saved because they are good people, or because of doing good works. Some people think that religious association saves them, or because they used to be an alter person, or their mother prayed a lot. A few don't believe they are saved. They may think they've done too much evil and don't think God can forgive them. Of course, many today don't even believe in life after death.

Always ask both questions. Many people think they're are already going to heaven, but when you ask them the second question, then you will see what that hope is based on. We are not looking for those who are already saved but the lost. Remember, always be loving; if they don't want to hear what you have to say then say, "Thank you for your time," or "God bless you" and move on. We are not here to convert people, just to be witnesses of Jesus (Acts 1:8). Pray that the Spirit will convict those who will receive Gods word.

Jesus came to save sinners and give them a hope. Ask them this next question:

Did you know that you can be 100% certain you are going to Heaven? Here's how (Go to 1 John 5:13):

(III)   Beside Romans 5:8 (somewhere on the same page) write Four Transitional Questions
1. Do you admit that you are a sinner?
2. Do you understand that sin separates you from God, now and in eternity?
3. Do you believe that Jesus died on the cross for your sins?

4. Would you like to be forgiven of all your sins and know you are going to Heaven?

This is so they can reflect and think about the scriptures that you have just shown them. They need to answer "yes" to these questions, or you really can't go on to the next step. Once they have said yes to them all and you reach the final question, proceed to show them Romans 10:9-13. After you read this passage in its original text first, then beside the word "whoever" in verse 13, you can substitute in the persons' name to make it more personal to them, and read that part to them again. So it would be that if John, or Susan, or David, or Janet should call upon the name of the LORD they shall be saved; that they can see that God is speaking directly to them.

(IV) **Five things to remember about leading a person to pray to invite Jesus into their heart:**

1. Always give and invitation - would you like to receive Jesus?
2. Always get them on their knees to pray, If it is possible.
3. You (the witness) pray first.
4. Stop your prayer before you say "Amen".
5. Break up the prayer of salvation for the sinner into short phrases.

The Pastor had a suggested prayer which the witness prays *after* presenting the Gospel (preferably with *both* on knees). Once you get the hang of what to say, then you can make it your own, this is just to help. It is not written in stone:

> *"Dear Heavenly Father, thank you for allowing me to share the Good News of how (the persons' name) can have a personal relationship with you and be 100% certain that he/she can go to Heaven when they die! Thank you for making forgiveness so easy. I am thankful that (persons' name) has a desire to know these things. Now, Holy Spirit, I ask you to convict persons' name of her/his sins. Help (person's name) to see how he/she is separated from you now and in eternity. Help (persons' name) to realize you want them to be your child and go to Heaven. You proved it by sending your only Son, Jesus, to die upon the cross for them. Help (persons' name) to see Jesus on that cross - suffering...bleeding...dying...because you love them! Help (persons' name) to feel you knocking on their heart's door. Give them the **faith** to believe you will save "whoever will call upon your name". That is what you said in your Word.*

Stop your prayer before you say "Amen" because once you say Amen, people tend to lift up their head and think they're finished. So when you stop before you say Amen, ask the person if they would like to receive Jesus at that time. If they say yes, ask them to repeat this prayer that I'm about to show you. Again, this is just to help it is not written in stone. You can type this prayer and tape it by Romans 10:9-13, to have it handy until you get the hang of it.

"Dear Jesus, I know I am a sinner. I believe you died for my sins and rose from the dead. I ask you to forgive me of all my sins. Come into my heart today and live forever. Give me a home in Heaven when I die. Help me to obey You! Thank you for hearing my prayer. Amen."

As soon as you finish the sinner's prayer, ask them if they meant that prayer they just said. If they did, then reassure them. "Then according to the Word of God where is Jesus right now? (Show them that He is in her/his heart) and that they're saved.

(V) Tell this new Christian how "to grow in the LORD" after they are saved:

1. **Read your Bible every day.** Ask this person if they have a Bible. If they don't, then give them one. Tell them to start reading in the Gospel of John, then 1 John and then read the entire New Testament.

1. **Teach them to pray to God every day.** Tell them to learn to take all their problems and needs to the LORD. One of the privileges of being saved is the right to pray.

2. **Tell them to start going to church every Sunday where the Bible and Holy Spirit are preached.**

Hebrews 10:25 says, "Do not forsake the assembling of yourselves together." Romans 10:17 says "Faith comes by hearing, and hearing by the Word of God". That is the reason that you should offer to come by and pick them up and bring them to church.

3. **Tell them to share their new faith in Jesus Christ with others.** Matthew 4:19 says, "Follow me and I'll make you fishers of men." Ask them: "Is there someone you know who will be happy to hear that you got saved? Call them and tell them!

4. **Teach the new Christian to make their salvation public by believer's baptism.** Turn and read Romans 6:4-6 and show them how that baptism pictured the death, burial, and resurrection of Jesus. Tell them that they should be baptized the first service that is available.

<u>Note:</u> Always leave the new convert a brochure from your church that gives the times of the services and the various ministries and the phone number. Call this new convert on Saturday to encourage and remind them of the services on Sunday.

This next part is something that Pastor Pritchard had recorded and transcribed to paper so we could see how it sounds when witnessing to someone. In the class we practiced and practiced with a partner until we felt comfortable with it. As you start to witness more and more to people, you make it your own. Practice with your loved ones, co-workers and neighbours and friends. You do not need to learn this word for word; it is just a guide:

> *"Did you know, you can know? In 1 John 5:13, the Bible says, 'These things have I written unto you that believe on the name of the Son of God; that you may know that you have eternal life.' And here's how you can know: in Romans 3:10, the Bible says, 'As it is written, There is none righteous, no not one,' and in verse 23, 'For all have sinned, and come short of the glory of God.' That means I'm a sinner and that means you are a sinner also."*
>
> *"Yes, I'm a sinner, also", the man responded.*
>
> *"Most people do not realize the seriousness of sin. God is a holy God and sin separates a sinner from God. This verse shows how serious sin is! In Romans 5:12 the Bible says, 'Wherefore as by one man sin entered into the world,' this means Adam committed the first sin, 'and death by sin; and so death passed upon all men, for all have sinned.' This word 'death' doesn't mean just dying and going to the grave; it means separation from God. Until our sins are forgiven, we are separated from God on this earth and will be separated from God in a lake of fire in hell forever and ever. This is our punishment for our sin.*
>
> *But the story doesn't end here! In Romans 6:23, the Bible says, 'For the wages of sin is death; but the gift of God is eternal life through Jesus Christ our LORD.'*

The Romans Road to Salvation

Being saved is a gift; it's absolutely free! You can't buy it, work for it, go to church for it, or be good for it. It is free! It would be as if a friend went to the store and purchased you a present. They paid for it, wrapped it, put a bow on it, and brought it to you. They did everything for you; all you have to do is receive it. That is what Jesus did! He left His home in Heaven, came to earth, died on the cross, shed His blood, and He paid for your sins. He did everything for you; all you have to do is receive it. And, Romans 5:8 says He did this for us while we were still sinners (he reads Romans 5:8). Most people think they have to stop doing everything bad before God will save them. But God loves us as sinners and Jesus died for us. He never did anything wrong. He left Heaven and died on the cross for you and me. When Jesus died for you, He made it possible for you to have forgiveness of sins and eternal life with God. But just because Jesus died for you that does not automatically save you. You must ask Jesus to save you.

Now, (persons' name) do you admit you are a sinner?"
"Yes."
"Do you understand that sin separated you from God?"
"Yes."
"Do you believe Jesus died on the cross for you?"
"Yes."
"Would you like to be forgiven of all your sins and know 100% you are going to Heaven?"
"Yes."
"Then, this is what you need to do. In Romans 10:9-13, the Bible says (read). Now 'whosoever' or 'whoever'

means you. We could substitute you name there, 'if (person's name) shall call upon the name of the LORD, (persons' name) shall be saved.' Do you think God would lie to you?"

"No."

"Then according to the Bible, if you asked Jesus into your heart right now, He would save you forever! Wouldn't you like this?"

"Yes."

"I want to pray with you before I leave (the witness prayer don't say Amen. yet). If you will trust Jesus to take you to Heaven when you die, just bow your head and close your eyes with me right now. If you mean this, with all you heart, pray this prayer after me: 'Dear Jesus, I know I am a sinner. I believe you died for my sins and rose from the dead. I ask you to forgive me of all my sins. Come into my heart today and live forever. Give me a home in Heaven when I die. Help me to obey you! Thank you for hearing my prayer. Amen.' (Always ask): did you mean that prayer?"

"Yes!"

"Then, according to the Bible, if you were to die today, where would you go?"

"Heaven!"

"That's right, for Romans says, 'For whosoever shall call upon the name of the LORD shall be saved.'"

It works, believe me - I have begun to win souls for Jesus. My prayer is that you too will see what God will do through you if you just step out in faith. You can't go wrong with what to say when you are using the Word of God.

Thanks, Pastor Pritchard and all the wonderful missionary saints that accompanied him. I thank the LORD for you. I want to encourage the readers that if you are ever in the Florida area stop in and worship with them at:

Grace Bible Church of Central Florida
(In the Pine Hills community)
801 Dorscher Road
Orlando, FL 32818
(407)-578-2085
www.GBCCF.ORG

The Romans Road to Salvation